Illustrated Handbook of General Science Teaching Aids

Illustrated Handbook of General Science Teaching Aids

JOHN ALUSIK

Parker Publishing Company, Inc.
West Nyack, New York

Library of Congress Cataloging in Publication Data

Alusik, John, (date)
    Illustrated handbook of general science teaching
aids.

    1. Science--Laboratory manuals. 2. Science--
Study and teaching (Secondary) I. Title.
Q161.2.A48   507'.8   72-10837
ISBN 0-13-451047-X

How This Book Will
Help You Teach Science
More Effectively

This illustrated handbook describes simple, effective science teaching aids you can make. Construction of the various devices lies well within the skills of the junior high school teacher. The materials used in every project are easily obtainable and in most cases relatively inexpensive.

To increase its utility value, the book is organized into various units of science instruction—and will group together the materials related to a specific unit. Construction diagrams give maximum clarity with the necessary measurements. Suggested materials are described in detail along with, in many cases, the source of supply. Photographs are used to supplement and further clarify the construction diagrams and will help insure a complete, detailed description of each project.

Everything in this book has been used repeatedly in classroom instruction over a ten-year period. Many of the projects were demonstrated by students during science shows as well as in the classrooms. Each project illustrates basic science concepts and can remain as a permanent part of science instruction program.

Learning in any subject area demands involvement. As is so often the case, the apparent science-shy student may possess manual skills which a teacher can utilize not only to motivate the student, but to provide him with an opportunity to make a significant contribution to the class. During the course of constructing many of the aids listed in this book, I often asked students in wood shop and metal shop classes to assist in various aspects of construction. On many occasions, students have made suggestions for changes as well as suggestions for substitution of materials. Problem solving was a continuous process during the construction phase, and in the process touched many areas outside of school and even involved parents, who frequently made significant contributions.

A shortage of funds sometimes limits the teacher's ability to purchase ready-made equipment that illustrates important scientific principles. This book not only helps the teacher overcome that problem, but will also bring greater student participation in making and using the various projects. There is a great range of possibilities insofar as variation or substitution of materials is concerned, and developing variations in some projects and materials can help the teacher easily bring about a tailor-made device to suit a particular classroom situation.

In summary, this book provides detailed, specific information about scientific teaching devices you can make and use in your classroom. It provides a sharp focus on each project, tells how to construct it—and even shows what it should look like when it is finished. Everything in this book is real, does work, and has been used many times in a large variety of classroom situations. You will find it a valuable working tool in developing more meaningful science teaching techniques, and in stimulating your students to a greater interest and participation in science.

John Alusik

Acknowledgments

The author wishes to express his appreciation to the following for their contributions of ideas and materials in the preparation of this manuscript:

Air Pollution Detector (Liquid Type)—Design taken from Popular Science Monthly, October 7, 1970, Popular Science Publishing Co., Inc.

Air Pollution Detector (Slide Type)—Air Pollution Experiments for Junior and Senior High School Science Classes, Air Pollution Control Association, Pittsburgh, Pennsylvania, 1969.

DNA Molecule—R. McKeeby, Union College, Cranford, New Jersey.

Geyser—Sourcebook for Geology and Earth Sciences, Robert L. Heller, Editor. Holt, Rinehart and Winston, Inc., N. Y.

Wind Tunnel—A Student Guide to Aeronautics, Merril E. Tower, Aero Publishers, Fallbrook, California.

Photographs by Ken Davis

This book is dedicated to all my past and present students. Some gave me ideas for materials in the book, others brought in raw materials used in making the teaching aids, many actually helped with the construction—and all helped motivate me to put this collection into book form.

Contents

4. Devices That Help You Teach Earth Science   • 47

Volcano . . . Permeability and Porosity . . . Water
Table . . . Profile Map Model . . . Magnetic Weather
Map . . . Crystal System Models . . . Fault Model
. . . Specific Gravity . . . Folded Mountains Model
. . . Flame Tests . . . Rainmaker . . . Centrifugal
Loop . . . Soil Horizons . . . Profile Models . . .
Mineral Identification . . . Cloud Maker . . . Sedi-
mentation Chamber . . . Stream Table . . . Geyser

5. Activities with Electrical Projects   • 79

Electrical Quizzer . . . Repulsion Coil . . . Overload
Demonstration . . . Magnets . . . High-Voltage Travel-
ing Arc . . . Magnetizer . . . Two-Way Light Circuit
. . . Magnetic Pile Driver . . . Electric Bell . . .
Conductors and Insulators . . . Telegraph . . . Quiz-
board . . . Circuits . . . Mechanical Generator . . .
Resistance Board . . . Door Chimes

6. Demonstrations with Heat   • 107

Explosion can . . . Expansion Bar . . . Molecular
Motion Demonstrator . . . Thermostat Demonstration
. . . Conductor Bar . . . Bell Thermostat

7. Ideas for Your Light Unit   • 119

Light Box . . . Polarization of Light . . . Rotating
Polarizer . . . Photoelectric Cell . . . Copy Box . . .
Pinhole Camera . . . Color by Addition

Illustrated Handbook
of General Science
Teaching Aids

chapter 1

Developing Projects That Teach about Air

Just as some animals live at the bottom of the sea, we live at the bottom of an ocean of air called the atmosphere. Like the animals of the sea who adapted to the crushing weight of water, man has adapted to the pressure of the air that extends from the earth's surface to the top of the atmosphere. If we could imagine a column of air with a surface area of 1 square inch extending over 20,000 miles high, we would record a pressure of 14.7 pounds on every square inch of surface at sea level.

Although air is a mixture of gases, man has learned how to use air to serve his purposes. We know that air can be compressed, as in an automobile tire, and we can create a difference of pressure to make a siphon work or a balloon rise. By understanding the nature and behavior of air, man has invented many mechanical devices that help him to improve his way of life and adjust to his environment.

On the following pages are a few ideas and devices you can construct that might help you understand the nature and behavior not only of air, but of objects that move through it.

It is left to your imagination how you can construct, vary, or adapt the following ideas to your satisfaction.

AIR PRESSURE

The apparatus shown in the illustration with the two gallon jugs is intended to provide the solution to the demonstration relating to the effect of air pressure on the surface of a liquid after it is displaced by water. It is suggested that the same apparatus (tubing, stoppers and funnel) be inserted in empty duplicator fluid cans and the demonstration begun just before the students enter the class. The objective here is an attempt to form a hypothesis leading to a solution. It is interesting to note the line of questioning taken by the students as to why water flows up the glass tubing. It is suggested that the teacher not participate in the discussion.

After a number of hypotheses are formed by the students, the teacher should place the apparatus using the jugs on the demonstration table to provide the solution. The students should conclude that the water poured into the lower can displaces air in the lower can. The air is forced up the tubing into the upper can where the air pressure on that liquid forces the liquid out of the upper can. The flow will stop when the top can is empty. To start the demonstration again, switch positions of the cans and pour water into the funnel again.

It is suggested that the experimenter use food coloring dye in the liquid in the one gallon jugs at the beginning of the demonstration.

Photo 1

AIR PRESSURE   DIAGRAM I

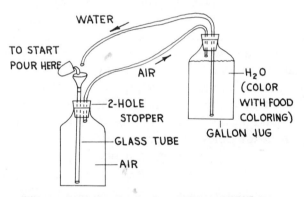

WATER

TO START
POUR HERE

AIR

H₂O
(COLOR
WITH FOOD
COLORING)

—2-HOLE
STOPPER

—GLASS TUBE

—AIR

GALLON JUG

POUR H₂O INTO FUNNEL TO BEGIN DEMONSTRATION.
WATER POURED INTO FUNNEL DISPLACES AIR IN THE
LOWER JUG.
AIR IS FORCED INTO UPPER JUG AND AIR PRESSURE
FORCES WATER OUT OF UPPER JUG.
PLACE UPPER JUG ABOUT 12" ABOVE LOWER JUG.
(THIS DEMONSTRATION CAN BE DONE BY USING
  DUPLICATOR FLUID CANS—AND HAVE STUDENTS
  DEVELOP A HYPOTHESIS.)

BERNOULLI'S PRINCIPLE

Very often students memorize Bernoulli's principle of air flow, but the vacuum cleaner motor provides an opportunity for the class to develop relationships that exist between Bernoulli's principle, air flow around the surface of an airplane wing, and air flow around a sphere.

Upon occasion I have used a very long extension cord and walked into the classroom with a 4-inch styrofoam sphere suspended in the air flow. The motor can be placed on the demonstration table and tilted slightly from the vertical and the sphere will remain suspended in the air flow.

It is suggested that an airplane wing cross-section be drawn on the chalkboard to illustrate the air flow pattern around the wing, with the higher pressure on the bottom of the wing and the lower pressure on the top surface of the wing resulting from increased velocity. Again it is suggested that an attempt be made to motivate the students in formulating a hypothesis. Spheres of various sizes and weights can be used as supplementary experiments after the concept is understood. Various tank-type vacuum cleaner motors are easily adapted to the demonstration. The motor must be completely enclosed in its housing. Be sure that the air intake at the base of the motor housing is free from obstruction at all times. A tapered portion of the handle can be inserted in the exit opening or a plastic pipe may be fitted in place.

Bernoulli's Principle—when a fluid (liquid or gas) is in steady flow, its pressure will be high wherever its velocity is low; and conversely, its pressure will be low wherever its velocity is high.

Photo 2

BERNOULLI'S PRINCIPLE DIAGRAM 2

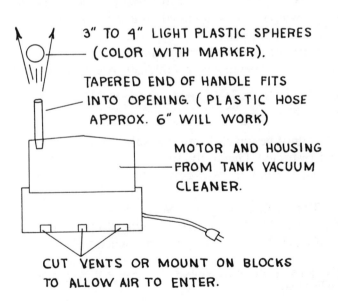

3" TO 4" LIGHT PLASTIC SPHERES (COLOR WITH MARKER).

TAPERED END OF HANDLE FITS INTO OPENING. (PLASTIC HOSE APPROX. 6" WILL WORK)

MOTOR AND HOUSING FROM TANK VACUUM CLEANER.

CUT VENTS OR MOUNT ON BLOCKS TO ALLOW AIR TO ENTER.

HOLD MOTOR WHEN TURNING ON SWITCH TO KEEP IT FROM TWISTING OFF TABLE.

WIND TUNNEL*

The wind tunnel provides unlimited opportunities for individual experimentation with models. In addition, it provides an opportunity for a group project to produce an inexpensive but durable teaching aid that can remain as a part of the science department teaching aids. It is suggested that the materials be collected and assembled in position before permanent mounting begins. A universal-type motor is recommended for use with a variable voltage source so that the speed of the motor can be varied during experiments. It is essential that a heavy wire screen be fastened at the rear of the fan housing for safety. This can be done very easily by cutting the wire to the height of the fan shaft, cutting a hole for the shaft, and lacing the cut wire with soft wire before fastening to the back of the housing.

In addition to the two experiments on the following pages, individual airplane models can be suspended in the airflow. Adjustable wing sections mounted on a scale can produce a measurable lift at various angles.

Cardboard models with movable rudder and aileron sections can be suspended on coathanger wire in the air flow.

(Ref. *Today's Basic Science*—Book 4—Harper & Row, TE p. 197)

It must be remembered that substitution of materials or sizes is not restricted. Generally, the size of the largest component (in this case the motor) will govern the overall size of the teaching aid.

The airplane wing section can be suspended on the angle of attack rods (⅛" hard wire). The wing section will "fly" in the air flow if it is held part way up the rods when the motor is turned on.

* The idea for this unit was inspired by reading *A Student Guide to Aeronautics*, Aero Publishers.

Photo 3

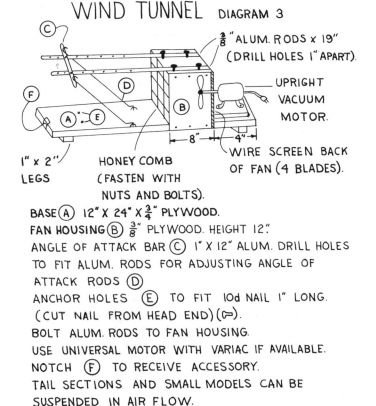

WIND TUNNEL DIAGRAM 3

$\frac{3}{8}$" ALUM. RODS x 19"
(DRILL HOLES 1" APART).

UPRIGHT
VACUUM
MOTOR.

WIRE SCREEN BACK
OF FAN (4 BLADES).

1" x 2"
LEGS

HONEY COMB
(FASTEN WITH
NUTS AND BOLTS).

BASE Ⓐ 12" X 24" X $\frac{3}{4}$" PLYWOOD.
FAN HOUSING Ⓑ $\frac{3}{8}$" PLYWOOD. HEIGHT 12".
ANGLE OF ATTACK BAR Ⓒ 1" X 12" ALUM. DRILL HOLES
TO FIT ALUM. RODS FOR ADJUSTING ANGLE OF
ATTACK RODS Ⓓ
ANCHOR HOLES Ⓔ TO FIT 10d NAIL 1" LONG.
(CUT NAIL FROM HEAD END) (☞).
BOLT ALUM. RODS TO FAN HOUSING.
USE UNIVERSAL MOTOR WITH VARIAC IF AVAILABLE.
NOTCH Ⓕ TO RECEIVE ACCESSORY.
TAIL SECTIONS AND SMALL MODELS CAN BE
SUSPENDED IN AIR FLOW.

Photo 4

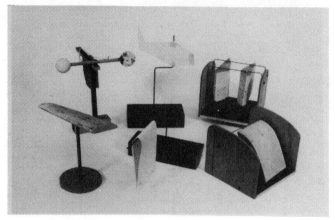

WIND TUNNEL ACCESSORIES DIAGRAM 4

<u>WING SECTION</u>
(FROM MODEL AIRPLANE)   FINE WIRE EYE HOOKS

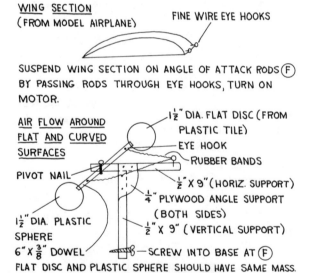

SUSPEND WING SECTION ON ANGLE OF ATTACK RODS Ⓕ
BY PASSING RODS THROUGH EYE HOOKS, TURN ON
MOTOR.

<u>AIR FLOW AROUND</u> $1\frac{1}{2}$" DIA. FLAT DISC (FROM
<u>FLAT AND CURVED</u>   PLASTIC TILE)
<u>SURFACES</u>   EYE HOOK

PIVOT NAIL   RUBBER BANDS

$\frac{1}{2}$" X 9" (HORIZ. SUPPORT)

$\frac{1}{4}$" PLYWOOD ANGLE SUPPORT
(BOTH SIDES)

$1\frac{1}{2}$" DIA. PLASTIC
SPHERE $\frac{1}{2}$" X 9" (VERTICAL SUPPORT)

6" X $\frac{3}{8}$" DOWEL   SCREW INTO BASE AT Ⓕ

FLAT DISC AND PLASTIC SPHERE SHOULD HAVE SAME MASS.
TIE EACH RUBBER BAND AT BACK EYE HOOK.
FASTEN RUBBER BANDS ON DOWEL STICK WITH EYE HOOKS.
GLUE SPHERE AND DISC TO DOWEL.
OIL PIVOT POINT.
PLACE SPHERE AND DISC ON BASE AT Ⓕ FACE INTO
AIRFLOW.

PROPELLER EFFECT

In this day of jet airplanes, many students have a very poor understanding of the purpose of the propeller when used on airplanes. In the demonstration model, two identical plastic propellers are mounted on dowel sticks and inserted at equal heights in front of and behind the motor-driven fan.

When the fan motor is turned on, students should observe the speed of rotation of each plastic propeller. With the fan motor still running, the plastic propeller positions should be reversed and observation made again.

In this demonstration, the fan acts as an airplane propeller to illustrate air flow in front of and behind the propeller. It should be understood that the purpose of the propeller is to produce the force that drives the plane forward (thrust). The propeller, rotated by a gas engine, forces the air around it backward. The air reacts by driving the propeller forward, producing the thrust.

Enclose the fan and motor with a large-holed wire screen for safety. If a calibrated stroboscope is available, the rotations of each plastic propeller can be compared.

Photo 5

PROPELLER EFFECT DIAGRAM 5

DRILL HOLES IN BASE FOR DOWELS.
CONSTRUCT SCREEN TO <u>COVER</u> FAN FOR SAFETY.
ALIGN SHAFT OF MOTOR AND PINS ON PLASTIC
PROPELLERS AT SAME HEIGHT.
OBSERVE EFFECT OF AIRFLOW ON PROPELLERS.

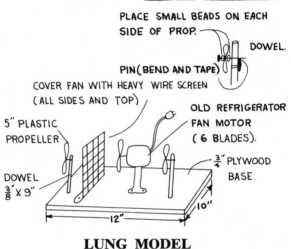

PROPELLER <u>CONSTRUCTION</u>

PLACE SMALL BEADS ON EACH
SIDE OF PROP.

DOWEL.

PIN(BEND AND TAPE)

COVER FAN WITH HEAVY WIRE SCREEN
(ALL SIDES AND TOP)

OLD REFRIGERATOR

5" PLASTIC
PROPELLER

FAN MOTOR
(6 BLADES).

$\frac{3}{4}$" PLYWOOD
BASE.

DOWEL
$\frac{3}{8}$" X 9"

10"

12"

LUNG MODEL

Regular movements of air into and from the lungs is called breathing. We breathe because of variations in air pressure. We can show this by means of a model, inexpensive to construct, but a good teaching aid that illustrates the parts of the body involved in the breathing process. The bottom of the gallon jug can be cut off, using the glass cutter device illustrated in this book. Because the glass in gallon jugs is usually uneven, it is suggested that the rough edges left after cutting be smoothed by using emery paper wrapped around a piece of wood block in place of fire polishing.

In addition to demonstrating how the lungs work, it is essential to point out the diaphragm, bronchial tubes, trachea, lungs, and chest cavity, and compare these parts and locations with those of the human body.

Photo 6

LUNG MODEL DIAGRAM 6

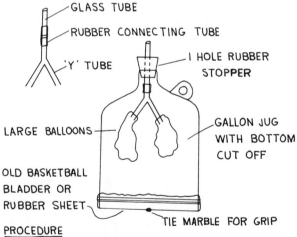

GLASS TUBE

RUBBER CONNECTING TUBE

'Y' TUBE

I HOLE RUBBER STOPPER

LARGE BALLOONS

GALLON JUG WITH BOTTOM CUT OFF

OLD BASKETBALL BLADDER OR RUBBER SHEET

TIE MARBLE FOR GRIP

PROCEDURE

PUT GLASS TUBE IN RUBBER STOPPER AND INSERT IN JUG.

COMPLETE LUNG ASSEMBLY AND CONNECT 'Y' TUBE TO GLASS TUBE AT RUBBER CONNECTING TUBE.

TAPE RUBBER SHEET TO BOTTOM OF JUG AFTER MARBLE IS TIED FOR GRIP.

LIFT PUMP

This lift pump was constructed as a result of frustration with broken models. Constructed from copper tubing and easily soldered, this model is almost indestructible. In addition, students can easily remove the piston and the #9 stopper to examine the construction and operation of the valves.

Before demonstrating this model, allow the piston (made from ⅛" plastic floor tile) and the #9 stopper to be submerged in water so that both valves (made of soft leather) can become pliable in order to work properly.

It is further recommended that a 2" inside diameter tube be used (if available). It will make construction of the valves easier. Also, an aluminum rod (⅜") is recommended as the piston rod. A larger cylinder requires a larger spout.

Mount the pump and permit students to actually operate the pump to experience the lifting force required. Compare this force to commercial models that apply the lever principle to lift the water. Discuss with the students how the pressure of the atmosphere on the surface of the well is used to push water up the pump to a limit of 34 feet.

(Ref. *Physics*—Taffel—Oxford Book Company)

Photo 7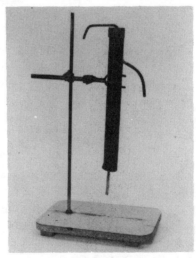

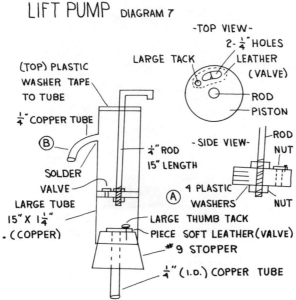

LIFT PUMP DIAGRAM 7

-TOP VIEW-

2-¼" HOLES

LARGE TACK   LEATHER
(VALVE)

(TOP) PLASTIC
WASHER TAPE
TO TUBE
¼" COPPER TUBE

ROD
PISTON

Ⓑ
ROD
NUT

SOLDER
VALVE
LARGE TUBE
15" X 1¼"
. (COPPER)

-SIDE VIEW-

¼" ROD
15" LENGTH

Ⓐ   4 PLASTIC
WASHERS   NUT

LARGE THUMB TACK
PIECE SOFT LEATHER (VALVE)
#9 STOPPER
¼" (I.D.) COPPER TUBE

MAKE PISTON WASHERS Ⓐ FROM ⅛" PLASTIC TILE.
VALVES MADE FROM SOFT LEATHER.
CUT PISTON FOR SMOOTH FIT IN LARGE TUBE.
SOAK VALVES IN WATER TO SOFTEN BEFORE USING.
SOLDER SPOUT Ⓑ 3½" FROM TOP.

FRICTIONLESS PUCK

The illustrated puck was a result of a class assignment to design a frictionless puck after a commercial model was demonstrated. Also, as part of the assignment, various surfaces and sizes of balloons were used to obtain the best results. Some balloons were too tall, causing the puck to tip over. Various surfaces such as desk tops, glass, and the floor were used in demonstrations.

It is recommended that a maximum limit be placed on the amount of money a student could spend on the assignment. The limit on this assignment was 15 cents. Best results were obtained on a glass plate (from an old 23" television).

Photo 8

FRICTIONLESS PUCK   DIAGRAM 8

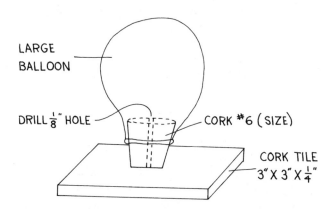

LARGE BALLOON

DRILL $\frac{1}{8}$" HOLE

CORK #6 (SIZE)

CORK TILE
3" X 3" X $\frac{1}{4}$"

GLUE CORK TO TILE (NARROW PART OF CORK IS
GLUED TO ROUGH SIDE OF TILE).
DRILL $\frac{1}{8}$" HOLE THROUGH CORK AND TILE.
STRETCH LARGE BALLOON OVER CORK.
INFLATE BALLOON FROM BOTTOM
RELEASE BALLOON ON SMOOTH SURFACE.
SIZE MAY VARY DEPENDING ON BALLOON.

chapter 2

Building Air Pollution Detectors

Although man and animals can survive for a limited period of time without food and water, survival without air is only a matter of a few minutes. An adult inhales about 400 cubic feet of air each day to obtain the oxygen necessary to sustain life. It is this fact that should make us realize that the air we breathe should not be a menace to health.

Pure, dry air is a mixture of gases; any other substances in the air, whether they are solid particles, vapors, or gases, are classified as contaminants. The effects of these contaminants are felt through loss of working days, deterioration of physical materials, and detrimental effects to vegetation.

Different varieties of pollens and spores released by fungi

and flowers are examples of natural pollutants. Man-made polution results from personal and industrial sources. Although governmental and personal concern about air pollution has been evident in the past few years, there appears to be an increasing need for skilled persons in every area to become involved in the air pollution problem.

In this chapter are illustrated some inexpensive experiments designed to acquaint students with air pollutants and the problems they present to each of us.

AIR POLLUTION

Air pollution experiments provide an opportunity for activities outside the classroom and in all parts of the community. The experiments can be conducted throughout the year and an analysis of air pollutants can be compiled after a period of time (fall, spring, winter, and summer). Shop students can become involved in the construction of the following air pollution detectors. The illustrations are intended to provide ideas, not only for construction and use, but for substitution of materials that will keep the cost of the detectors near zero.

Prior to any experiments with the detectors, microscope slides of carbon particles (from a chimney or car exhaust), dust particles, pollen, particles from burning leaves, and cigarette ashes should be made by the students for future reference. After collecting samples with the detectors, students can compare the collected particles with the reference set.

The detectors are easily carried and set up. After exposure, they should be covered by a clean plastic bag when being returned to the classroom.

CELLOPHANE TAPE DETECTOR

The cellophane tape detector enables the student to place this device at a specific location for extended periods of time without supervision. The detector should be oriented (N-S or E-W) to provide an indication of directional flow of the pollutants.

After exposure, the tape is removed and fastened face down on microscope slides. The slides should be identified as to their location and exposure time and viewed through a microscope. Students should refer to a set of prepared slides in attempting to identify the type of pollutants collected on the cellophane tape. Hypotheses should be formed in an attempt to identify the source of the pollutants.

Photo 9

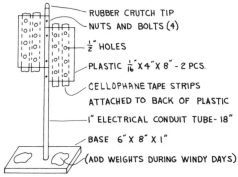

AIR POLLUTION   DIAGRAM 9
CELLOPHANE TAPE DETECTOR

- RUBBER CRUTCH TIP
- NUTS AND BOLTS (4)
- $\frac{1}{2}''$ HOLES
- PLASTIC $\frac{1}{16}'' \times 4'' \times 8''$ - 2 PCS.
- CELLOPHANE TAPE STRIPS ATTACHED TO BACK OF PLASTIC
- 1" ELECTRICAL CONDUIT TUBE- 18"
- BASE 6" X 8" X 1"
- (ADD WEIGHTS DURING WINDY DAYS)

TAPE BOTH PIECES OF PLASTIC AND DRILL HOLES.
HAVE DETECTOR FACE INTO WIND.
REMOVE PLASTIC STRIPS AND PLACE FACE DOWN
ON SLIDE.
OBSERVE UNDER MICROSCOPE.
COVER WITH PLASTIC BAG WHEN EXPOSURE
IS COMPLETED.

STICK-TAPE DETECTOR

This inexpensive detector enables the student to determine the prevailing flow of air pollutants when the detector is oriented with a compass. Two jars are mounted at right angles to each other and the top jar is mounted inversely. The top jar results should verify the pollutants collected by the two side-mounted jars. The results, in this experiment, are observed by a hand lens. Again, location and direction are important in determining pollution patterns as well as identification of pollutants.

Photo 10

AIR POLLUTION DIAGRAM 10
STICK-TAPE DETECTOR

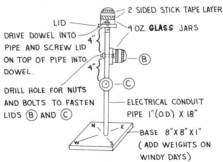

2 SIDED STICK TAPE LAYER

LID

DRIVE DOWEL INTO
PIPE AND SCREW LID
ON TOP OF PIPE INTO
DOWEL.

4 OZ. **GLASS** JARS

Ⓑ

ⓒ

DRILL HOLE FOR NUTS
AND BOLTS TO FASTEN
LIDS Ⓑ AND ⓒ

ELECTRICAL CONDUIT
PIPE 1"(O.D.) X 18"

BASE 8"X 8"X 1"
(ADD WEIGHTS ON
WINDY DAYS)

PLACE B AND C JARS AT 90° TO EACH OTHER.
PLACE 2 STRIPS (2-SIDE STICK) TAPE ON EACH JAR.
ORIENT DIRECTION (NORTH ON DETECTOR POINTING
NORTH).
EXPOSE DETECTOR DESIRED LENGTH OF TIME.
OBSERVE WITH HAND LENS.
CONDUIT PIPE FITS INTO HOLE IN BASE.

SLIDE DETECTOR

This type of detector collects pollutants directly on a vaseline-coated glass slide which can be viewed with a microscope. In addition to the experiments that can be conducted with the stick-tape and cellophane tape detectors, this detector can be suspended at various heights by removing the base and the iron pipe support. A simple hook can be made to fasten through the pegboard and permit fastening to objects at various heights.

It is recommended that at least two aluminum slide holders be made for each detector and they should be mounted tangent to each other to give the best possible coverage.

Both masonite boards are circular with threaded rods mounted at 120° angles. The slide holders are easily mounted in the masonite holes. The slides can be viewed under a microscope or bioscope, if available, under both high and low power.

Photo 11

Reproduced with permission from *Air Pollution Experiments for Junior and Senior High School Sciences Classes,* Air Pollution Control Association, Pittsburgh, 1969.

SLIDE DETECTOR DIAGRAM II

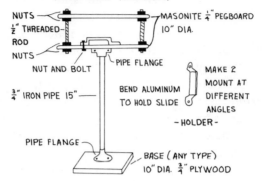

MICROSCOPE SLIDE HOLDER
(FROM SCRAP ALUMINUM)

NUTS — MASONITE $\frac{1}{4}$" PEGBOARD
$\frac{1}{2}$" THREADED— 10" DIA.
ROD
NUTS
NUT AND BOLT — PIPE FLANGE
$\frac{3}{4}$" IRON PIPE 15" — BEND ALUMINUM MAKE 2
TO HOLD SLIDE MOUNT AT
DIFFERENT
ANGLES
– HOLDER –

PIPE FLANGE
BASE (ANY TYPE)
10" DIA. $\frac{3}{4}$" PLYWOOD

NEED: 3 THREADED RODS 8" LENGTH PLACED 120° APART.
2 PCS. 10" DIA. $\frac{1}{4}$" PEGBOARD.
2 PIPE FLANGES.
12 NUTS TO HOLD MASONITE IN PLACE.
PROCEDURE:
COAT EACH SLIDE WITH PETROLEUM JELLY.
EXPOSE DETECTOR.
OBSERVE SLIDES UNDER MICROSCOPE.

MOTOR-DRIVEN DETECTOR

A more challenging but still inexpensive detector is constructed using a motor obtained from a tank vacuum cleaner (Electrolux works very well) mounted on a base. Although limited for outdoor use, this device was intended primarily for collecting indoor samples of pollutants.

The can (1 pound key-type lid) is fastened to the motor cover with small bolts. The collecting device here is a piece of filter paper held in place by two aluminum washers (made from aluminum scraps) and a wire screen that prevents the paper from collapsing.

It is suggested that the motor be run intermittently when collecting samples. It is also suggested that more than one interchangeable lid be constructed for easy operation or change of location. The particles collected are viewed with a hand lens for identification.

Photo 12

MOTOR DRIVEN DETECTOR DIAGRAM 12

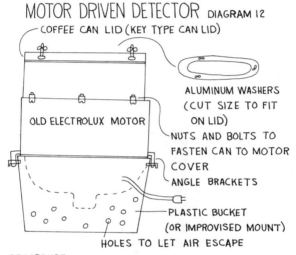

COFFEE CAN LID (KEY TYPE CAN LID)

ALUMINUM WASHERS
(CUT SIZE TO FIT
ON LID)

OLD ELECTROLUX MOTOR

NUTS AND BOLTS TO
FASTEN CAN TO MOTOR
COVER

ANGLE BRACKETS

PLASTIC BUCKET
(OR IMPROVISED MOUNT)

HOLES TO LET AIR ESCAPE

PROCEDURE:

CUT HOLE IN LID OF COFFEE CAN TO DESIRED SIZE.
CUT 2 ALUMINUM WASHERS TO FIT ON LID WITH
SAME SIZE AS HOLE IN LID.
CUT SCREEN WIRE SAME SIZE AS WASHERS.
PLACE IN FOLLOWING ORDER (TOP-DOWN)
 WASHER- FILTER PAPER- SCREEN- CAN LID- WASHER
BOLT WITH 3 NUTS AND BOLTS.
EXPOSE DETECTOR BY RUNNING MOTOR AT 5 MINUTE
INTERVALS.
REMOVE FILTER PAPER AND OBSERVE WITH HAND LENS.
(I MOUNTED MOTOR IN PLASTIC BUCKET FOR
STUDENT PROTECTION. ANY SUBSTITUTE MOUNTING
O.K.)

LIQUID-TYPE COLLECTOR

Although similar to the motor-driven detector, the pollutants here are collected in a liquid bath. After collection, the liquid can be placed on a concavity slide and viewed with a microscope. With reasonable care, the liquid can be allowed to evaporate and the solid particles collected from the evaporating dish and again viewed with a hand lens or a microscope. Another option is that the liquid can be filtered and observed with a hand lens.

It is essential that the motor be thoroughly cleaned prior to operation. This can be done by running the motor with the jar removed, or by forcing air through the motor. Service station attendants usually are cooperative in performing this small service.

Photo 13

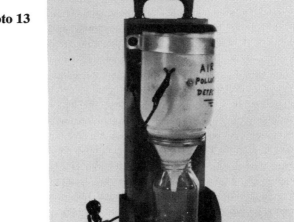

Design taken from *Popular Science Monthly,* October 1970, © Popular Science Publishing Co., Inc.

LIQUID-TYPE COLLECTOR DIAGRAM 13

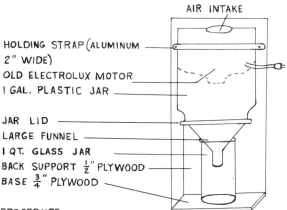

AIR INTAKE

HOLDING STRAP (ALUMINUM 2" WIDE)
OLD ELECTROLUX MOTOR
1 GAL. PLASTIC JAR

JAR LID
LARGE FUNNEL
1 QT. GLASS JAR
BACK SUPPORT $\frac{1}{2}$" PLYWOOD
BASE $\frac{3}{4}$" PLYWOOD

PROCEDURE:
MOUNT MOTOR IN PLASTIC JAR AND FASTEN TO BACK SUPPORT.
CUT HOLE IN PLASTIC JAR LID TO FIT FUNNEL (A LARGE ALUMINUM WASHER MAY BE NEEDED TO HOLD FUNNEL IN PLACE).
OBTAIN   25 ML ALCOHOL (ISOPROPYL)
　　　　　25 ML H_2O (MIX BOTH)
POUR SOLUTION INTO GLASS JAR AND RUN DETECTOR FOR 5 MIN. INTERVALS.
SWIRL SOLUTION IN GLASS JAR AND POUR INTO SMALL JARS. USE CONCAVITY SLIDE AND OBSERVE WITH MICROSCOPE.
(SOLUTION MAY BE FILTERED AND OBSERVED WITH HAND LENS).

CAR VACUUM DETECTOR

With today's focus on car pollution, the car vacuum adapts readily to sampling activities. All that is necessary is to remove the cone-shaped dust collector and insert a piece of filter paper supported by a piece of wire screen. The cone-shaped dust collector is removed when the vacuum is taken apart. The detector can be used to sample various car exhausts simply by plugging the wire into the cigarette lighter socket. The sample should be obtained with the motor of the car running for a few minutes. Care must be taken by the student not to remain too close to the car exhaust.

It is interesting to make a comparative study of samples obtained from cars equipped with pollution reducing devices and cars without these devices. It is essential that a list of variables be made that might affect the results. Among these would be tune-up, regular and premium gas, model of car, etc.

Photo 14

CAR VACUUM POLLUTION DETECTOR

DIAGRAM 14

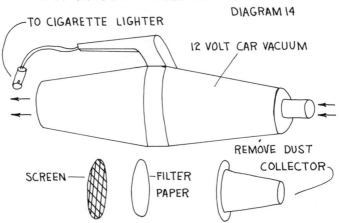

TO CIGARETTE LIGHTER

12 VOLT CAR VACUUM

REMOVE DUST COLLECTOR

SCREEN — FILTER PAPER

UNSCREW VACUUM CLEANER AND REMOVE DUST COLLECTOR.
INSERT FILTER PAPER WITH WIRE SCREEN BACK.
PLUG CLEANER INTO CIGARETTE LIGHTER.
AIR SAMPLES AND EXHAUST SAMPLES OF DIFFERENT CARS CAN BE COLLECTED.

chapter 3

Understanding Chemistry
with Models

All substances exist as elements or compounds. Compounds consist of different elements which are chemically combined. Understanding chemistry presents a problem of the invisible nature of the fundamental particles. Another existing difficulty is that explanations for many chemical phenomena are not available.

A model is a physical device that attempts to explain the structure or behavior of a substance. During the course of time, many models have been made and many changes (mathematical and physical) have been made as new knowledge is obtained. Understanding the structure of a model enables one to make predictions concerning its physical and chemical nature.

By constructing and observing models, a student can develop an understanding of the physical and chemical properties of a compound. The models illustrated on the following pages describe some elementary compounds and the bonds that hold them together. The chemical equations model illustrates the kind and number of atoms involved in the simple chemical reactions and their rearrangement in the products of the chemical reactions.

WATER MOLECULE

To help him understand the behavior of matter, the chemist often constructs a physical model. The three-dimensional water model pictured in this book attempts to illustrate the following concepts:

The Nucleus—composed of protons and neutrons

Electrons—orbit around the nucleus

Orbitals— 1s-oxygen—containing 2 electrons

2s-oxygen—containing 2 electrons

3-2p oxygen—two containing 1 electron each and one containing 2 electrons

1s-hydrogen—containing one electron and bonded to a 2p orbital that contains only one electron. (This bond is duplicated by the other hydrogen atom.)

It must be remembered that any individual orbital can contain a maximum of two electrons.

The primary objective of this model is to introduce the concept that the atom is three-dimensional, not two-dimensional as pictured in this book.

In constructing the water molecule, it is suggested that one-inch spheres be used for protons and neutrons and ¾-inch spheres for the electrons. Coloring the various orbitals with paint helps to identify each orbital. Painting should be done after the model is completely assembled.

A hole may be drilled into the spheres (electrons) and placed on the wire. Slide the spheres away from the area being soldered and return and glue when soldering is completed.

Photo 15

WATER MOLECULE DIAGRAM 15

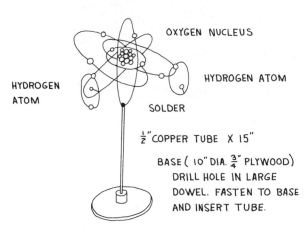

OXYGEN NUCLEUS

HYDROGEN ATOM

HYDROGEN ATOM

SOLDER

$\frac{1}{2}$" COPPER TUBE X 15"

BASE (10" DIA. $\frac{3}{4}$" PLYWOOD)
DRILL HOLE IN LARGE
DOWEL. FASTEN TO BASE
AND INSERT TUBE.

ORBITALS- MADE FROM #10 COPPER WIRE
ELECTRONS- USE $\frac{3}{4}$" STYRENE SPHERES.
(COLOR FIRST) DRILL HOLE AND INSERT ON WIRE.
TIE WIRES TOGETHER WITH FINE WIRE BEFORE
SOLDERING.
SIZE OF MODEL DEPENDS UPON SIZE OF SPHERES
AVAILABLE. (I USED $\frac{1}{2}$" SPHERES FOR NUCLEUS
AND $\frac{3}{4}$" SPHERES FOR ELECTRONS)

MOLECULAR MODELS

The construction of molecular models presents an activity well within the reach of the elementary as well as the junior and senior high schools. Atoms combine in certain ways to form molecules. Valence is a measure of the ability of an atom to combine with other atoms, and the concept of valence is illustrated by the number of connecting sticks. One stick between two spheres indicates that one pair of electrons is being shared by the atoms connected to the stick.

The focus here is on constructing molecules of common substances. If possible, different sizes of spheres should be used as well as a color coding system. It is suggested that students develop the concept of the writing of formulas to identify their models.

Photo 16

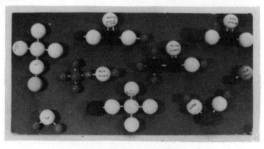

MOLECULAR MODELS I DIAGRAM 16

WATER - H_2O

HYDROGEN PEROXIDE - H_2O_2

CARBON MONOXIDE - CO

CARBON DIOXIDE - CO_2

AMMONIUM HYDROXIDE VINEGAR
NH_4OH CH_3COOH

COLOR CODE:
H - HYDROGEN (RED)   Na - SODIUM (SILVER)
O - OXYGEN (WHITE)   Mg - MAGNESIUM (GREY)
C - CARBON (BLACK)   Ca - CALCIUM (BROWN)
N - NITROGEN (BLUE)   S - SULFUR (YELLOW)
                      Cl - CHLORINE (GREEN)

MOLECULAR MODELS II DIAGRAM 17

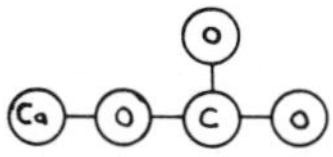

CALCIUM CARBONATE
$CaCO_3$

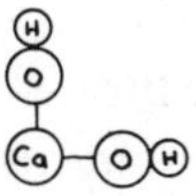

CALCIUM HYDROXIDE
$Ca(OH)_2$

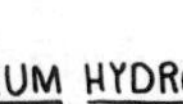

SODIUM CHLORIDE
$NaCl$

SODIUM HYDROXIDE
$NaOH$

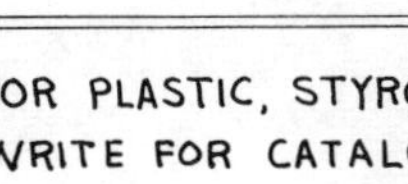

SODIUM HYDROGEN CARBONATE
$NaHCO_3$

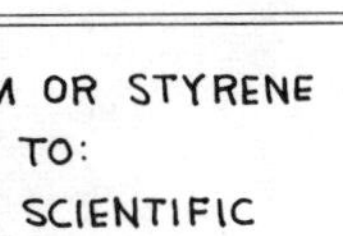

MAGNESIUM SULFATE
$MgSO_4$

FOR PLASTIC, STYROFOAM OR STYRENE SPHERES,
WRITE FOR CATALOGUE TO:
EDMUND SCIENTIFIC
BARRINGTON, N.J.

CHEMICAL REACTIONS MODELS

Equations and models for chemical reactions attempt to explain what actually happens. Entering the chemical reactions are the "reactants," and the results of the chemical change in the new combinations of atoms are the "products." It must be remembered that in a chemical reaction no atoms have been destroyed and no new atoms created. Observe the chemical reactions model; the same number and kind of atoms appear in the reactants and in the products. Only their combinations have changed.

There are four main types of reactions in elementary chemistry, as illustrated by the model and explained below:

1. Composition—two or more substances combine to form a more complex substance.

2. Decomposition—a complex substance is broken down to form two or more simpler substances.

3. Single replacement—one substance is displaced from its compound by another substance.

4. Double replacement—two or more substances exchange places.

Photo 18

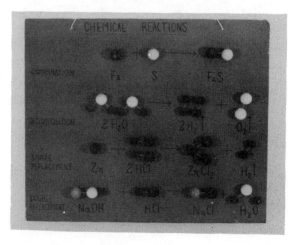

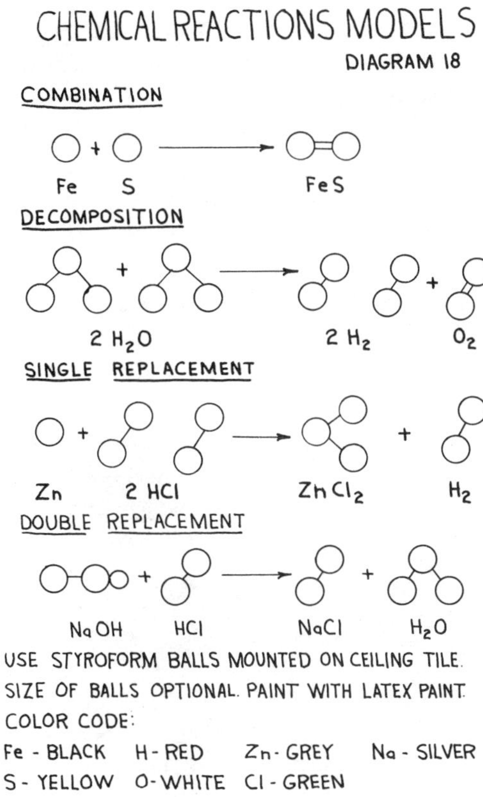

CHEMICAL REACTIONS MODELS

DIAGRAM 18

COMBINATION

Fe + S ⟶ FeS

DECOMPOSITION

2 H_2O ⟶ 2 H_2 + O_2

SINGLE REPLACEMENT

Zn + 2 HCl ⟶ $ZnCl_2$ + H_2

DOUBLE REPLACEMENT

NaOH + HCl ⟶ NaCl + H_2O

USE STYROFORM BALLS MOUNTED ON CEILING TILE.
SIZE OF BALLS OPTIONAL. PAINT WITH LATEX PAINT.
COLOR CODE:

Fe - BLACK   H - RED   Zn - GREY   Na - SILVER
S - YELLOW   O - WHITE   Cl - GREEN

ELECTROLYTE INDICATOR

Using the conductivity apparatus, an electrical source is connected in series with a light bulb and a pair of electrodes. The solution to be tested is placed in a glass container and the electrodes are dipped into the solution. If the substance is an electrolyte, the current will pass through the solution and the bulb will light.

Not all electrolytes are equally good conductors of electricity, and these can be tested by preparing solutions of various substances listed in the diagram. Acids, bases, and salts are classes of compounds that are electrolytes. Compounds that ionize when dissolved in water and conduct electricity are called electrolytes.

Sugar, alcohol, glycerine, and pure water are examples of non-electrolytes. If available, a light meter can give a more accurate reading of the conductivity of the solutions. Students can graph the conductivity of the solution if a light measuring device is available.

When a substance is dissolved in water, some of its molecules break up into positively or negatively charged ions. An ion is an atom or group of atoms that has an electric charge. Any solution that contains these positively and negatively charged ions is able to conduct an electric current and is therefore called an electrolyte. Acids, bases, and salts when dissolved in water are examples of electrolytes.

Photo 19

ELECTROLYTE INDICATOR DIAGRAM 19
(IONIZATION)

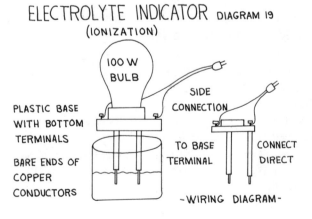

100 W BULB

PLASTIC BASE WITH BOTTOM TERMINALS

BARE ENDS OF COPPER CONDUCTORS

SIDE CONNECTION

TO BASE TERMINAL

CONNECT DIRECT

—WIRING DIAGRAM—

USE # 16 INSULATED COPPER WIRE.
TEST FOR COMPLETE CIRCUIT BY TOUCHING BARE
ENDS OF CONDUCTORS WITH INSULATED
SCREW DRIVER.
MAKE 10% SOLUTIONS OF THE FOLLOWING:

HCl	NaOH	H_2O
H_2SO_4	NH_4OH	NaCl
$HC_2H_3O_2$	$C_{12}H_{22}O_{11}$	$CuSO_4$

CANDLE GASES

The activity of observing a candle flame suggests an introductory lesson in chemistry. In addition to identifying the different cones, the students can attempt to collect unburned gas and pipe it off by using a piece of copper tubing and igniting the unburned gases. The "reamed" end of the copper tubing is placed in the center (dark) cone and escaping gases will begin to flow from the opposite end, which can be ignited. Care must be taken that air currents in the classroom be reduced to a minimum.

Photo 20

CANDLE GASES

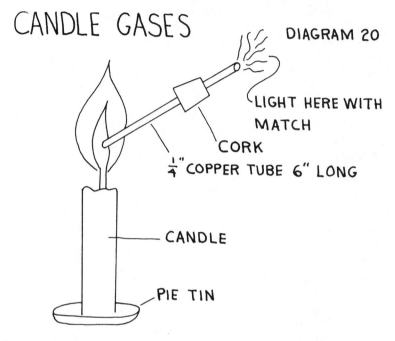

DIAGRAM 20

LIGHT HERE WITH
MATCH

CORK

$\frac{1}{4}$" COPPER TUBE 6" LONG

CANDLE

PIE TIN

REAMED END OF COPPER TUBE PLACED IN FLAME <u>ONLY</u>.
CORK IS USED FOR HOLDING OR PLACING IN
CLAMP ON RING STAND.
PIE TIN COLLECTS MELTED WAX.
USE TUBING CUTTER ON COPPER TUBE.

chapter 4

Devices That Help You
Teach Earth Science

The study of earth science is made easier because each of us lives in a natural laboratory for the subject. Although the laboratory has its limitations (nearness of volcanoes, glaciers, etc.), many real conditions do exist that present opportunities for investigation.

Throughout the long history of the earth, powerful forces have shaped and reshaped the earth's surface. All the many forms of the earth's surface (hills, mountains, valleys, and plains) are the results of forces working above and beneath the earth's surface. Pressures beneath the earth's surface cause the crust to fold, warp, bend, and break. Volcanoes build new mountains while running water never ceases its work of eroding everything it comes in contact with. Even today the crust of the earth is changing. It is possible that in the distant future the old continents may project above the present oceans.

The activities of the following pages of this chapter present an opportunity to the student to investigate conditions he finds in his immediate environment, and to construct materials that could produce an artificial situation for further investigations of conditions not readily available.

Ideas for many of the teaching aids illustrated in this chapter were suggested by students, and some students helped in the construction. Correspondence with students in other states led to an exchange of materials and ideas that were also incorporated in the chapter.

VOLCANO

A volcanic hill or mountain is the result of molten rock that comes to the surface from an opening in the earth's crust. Most volcanoes are built up of layers of lava and volcanic ash. Magma, hot liquid rock, is the parent of all igneous rocks.

Any explanation of volcanic activity involves the problem of heat. Although the source of volcanic heat is not completely understood, it is probably a combination of radioactive elements in the earth's crust, heat from the interior of the earth, and heat produced from the pressure of overlaying rocks.

The model can be used as a good introductory demonstration for a geology unit. The ammonium dichromate can be easily ignited with a wooden match to illustrate the eruption of a volcano. The demonstration of burning the ammonium dichromate can be explained by the following chemical reaction:

$$(NH_4)_2 Cr_2 O_7 \rightarrow 2CrO_3 + (NH_3)_2 \uparrow + H_2O \uparrow$$

The demonstration can lead into a discussion of the formation and composition of igneous rocks. Magnesium turnings can be added to the ammonium dichromate to increase the burning activity and produce eruptions during burning.

Photo 21

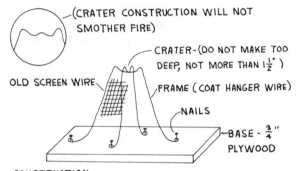

VOLCANO   DIAGRAM 21

(CRATER CONSTRUCTION WILL NOT SMOTHER FIRE)

CRATER-(DO NOT MAKE TOO DEEP, NOT MORE THAN $1\frac{1}{2}''$)

OLD SCREEN WIRE

FRAME (COAT HANGER WIRE)

NAILS

BASE - $\frac{3}{4}''$ PLYWOOD

<u>CONSTRUCTION</u>

MAKE FRAME FROM COAT HANGER WIRE AND NAIL TO BASE. WRAP OLD SCREENWIRE AROUND FRAME AND LACE TO FRAME WITH SCRAPS OF SOFT WIRE. STAPLE SCREEN TO BASE.

USE PLASTER OF PARIS TO COVER SCREEN. DO NOT MAKE FIRST COAT TOO WET.- IT WILL GO THROUGH SCREEN.

LET DRY AND SPRAY PAINT.

SIZE MAY VARY. (MINE IS 15" HIGH - CRATER 2" DIA.- 1" DEEP.)

USE AMMONIUM DICHROMATE WITH MAGNESIUM TURNINGS FOR ERUPTION. IGNITE WITH WOOD MATCH.

PERMEABILITY AND POROSITY

Permeability is a rock's capacity for transmitting a fluid. Coarse-grained sand and gravel allow water to pass through easily. In the experiment, different sized particles can be separated by using screens of various sizes. Equal volumes (100 ml) should be placed in different containers and an equal volume of water (100 ml) should be poured through the substance. Students should record the length of time it takes for the volume of water to pass through the different substances. The results can be illustrated with a graph.

Porosity is the amount of open spaces in rock or earth material. The shape of the mineral grains determines how porous a rock will be. (Ability to store water between the mineral grains.) Spherical particles of uniform size have the capacity for storing more water than most other rock forms.

In the experiment, the students should bring in their own samples (approximately 1½ inches square) and identify them. The rock is weighed and placed in a measured volume of water. After about 48 hours, the student should remove the rock sample

Photo 22

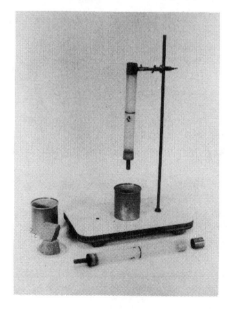

and again weigh it. The remaining volume of water should be measured. Care must be taken to prevent evaporation while the rock remains submerged in a container. This is easily done by using a container with a plastic lid.

Various rock samples can be used to form comparisons and conclusions. There is a definite relationship between the amount of water absorbed by the rock and its increase in weight.

Common rocks, such as sandstone, shale, basalt, calcite, etc., are used for this experiment.

PERMEABILITY - POROSITY DIAGRAM 22

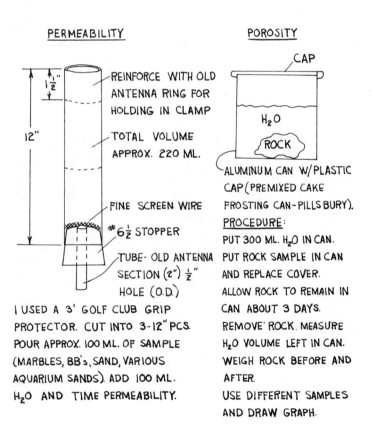

PERMEABILITY

POROSITY

REINFORCE WITH OLD ANTENNA RING FOR HOLDING IN CLAMP

$1\frac{1}{2}$"

12"

TOTAL VOLUME APPROX. 220 ML.

FINE SCREEN WIRE

#$6\frac{1}{2}$ STOPPER

TUBE- OLD ANTENNA SECTION (2") $\frac{1}{2}$" HOLE (O.D.)

I USED A 3' GOLF CLUB GRIP PROTECTOR. CUT INTO 3-12" PCS. POUR APPROX. 100 ML. OF SAMPLE (MARBLES, BB's, SAND, VARIOUS AQUARIUM SANDS). ADD 100 ML. H_2O AND TIME PERMEABILITY.

CAP

H_2O

ROCK

ALUMINUM CAN W/PLASTIC CAP (PREMIXED CAKE FROSTING CAN-PILLSBURY).
PROCEDURE:
PUT 300 ML. H_2O IN CAN.
PUT ROCK SAMPLE IN CAN AND REPLACE COVER.
ALLOW ROCK TO REMAIN IN CAN ABOUT 3 DAYS.
REMOVE ROCK. MEASURE H_2O VOLUME LEFT IN CAN.
WEIGH ROCK BEFORE AND AFTER.
USE DIFFERENT SAMPLES AND DRAW GRAPH.

WATER TABLE

The term water table is commonly used to describe the upper surface or a zone of saturation within the earth. The level of the ground-water is affected by the amount of rainfall, amount of evaporation, and the permeability of the rocks. The rise of the water table following a period of rainfall is also affected by the runoff of the rainfall and absorption by vegetation.

Any large glass container can be used to show the rise and fall of the water table. A mixture of sand and gravel can be placed in an aquarium (5 gallon) or a 1-gallon glass jar. A zone of saturation can be seen through the glass. By placing a plastic tube (1½-inch diameter) in the sand near the bottom of the container, a siphon can be used to remove the water from the tube (which represents a well). Holes may be drilled in the side of the tube and cotton cloth wrapped and held in place with rubber bands will prevent particles from filling the well.

Photo 23

WATER TABLE DEMONSTRATION DIAGRAM 23

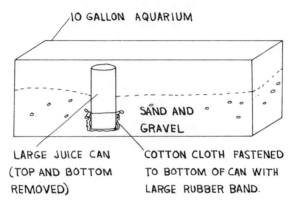

10 GALLON AQUARIUM

SAND AND GRAVEL

LARGE JUICE CAN
(TOP AND BOTTOM
REMOVED)

COTTON CLOTH FASTENED
TO BOTTOM OF CAN WITH
LARGE RUBBER BAND.

PROCEDURE:

POUR H_2O INTO AQUARIUM TO SATURATE SAND AND
GRAVEL.

H_2O WILL FLOW INTO JUICE CAN.

BY REMOVING H_2O WITH A LADEL OR SMALL PUMP
(A SIPHON WORKS WELL ALSO), THE MOVEMENT
OF THE WATER TABLE CAN BE OBSERVED.

PROFILE MAP MODEL

A profile of a topographic map is a two-dimensional representation of a generally small area of the earth's surface. The ups and downs on a topographic map are usually shown by means of symbols, called contour lines.

The model makes an attempt to illustrate how a profile is drawn from a contour map. The possibility here for substituting materials is unlimited. Different colors were used to illustrate different contour elevations (top part) and corresponding colors were used to illustrate the elevation in the profile (bottom part).

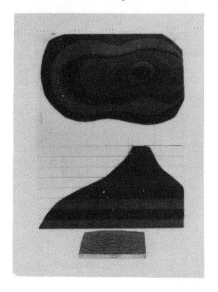

Photo 24

PROFILE MAP MODEL   DIAGRAM 24

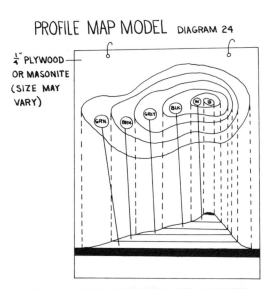

$\frac{1}{4}$" PLYWOOD
OR MASONITE
(SIZE MAY
VARY)

CONTOUR LAYERS WERE MADE WITH DIFFERENT
COLORED PIECES OF INDOOR-OUTDOOR CARPET.
THE CORRESPONDING ELEVATION LAYERS WERE
MADE OF THE SAME COLOR. THE LAYERS WERE
PASTED TO THE PLYWOOD OR MASONITE WITH
CARPET CEMENT.

MAGNETIC WEATHER MAP

The magnetic weather map provides a daily activity not only for plotting the daily weather conditions, but for predicting the weather as well. If the weather map is approximately 3 feet square in size or larger and magnetic strips are available, the high and low pressure areas can be plotted by using small pieces of magnetic strips to serve as arrows. If the available size is less than 3' x 3', it is suggested that small magnets be used to hold in place symbols indicating weather conditions existing in different areas. It is also recommended that the map projected include some of Canada (origin of cold air masses) and part of the Gulf of Mexico (origin of tropical maritime air masses).

Photo 25

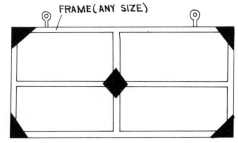

MAGNETIC WEATHER MAP DIAGRAM 25

FRAME (ANY SIZE)

PROCEDURE:
MAKE FRAME FROM 1" X 2" PCS.
REINFORCE CORNERS WITH $\frac{1}{4}$" PLYWOOD SCRAPS.

NAIL THIN GAUGE SHEET METAL ON FRAME.
PROJECT MAP OF N. AMERICA (USE OPAQUE PROJECTOR)
ON PLASTIC WINDOW SHADE. OUTLINE STATES
WITH FINE-POINT MARKER.
STAPLE MAP TO FRAME (MAP GOES AROUND TO
SIDES OF FRAME).
MAGNETIC STRIPS ADHERE TO SHEET METAL.
WEATHER CONDITIONS CAN BE HELD IN PLACE
BY INDIVIDUAL SMALL MAGNETS.

CRYSTAL SYSTEM MODELS

There are six different systems of crystals, varying according to the angles between their faces. When a mineral grows without interference, it is bounded by plane surfaces systematically arranged, giving it a characteristic crystal form. Its crystal form is the external expression of its internal crystalline structure. The faces of crystals are composed of surface layers of atoms or ions. The size of the faces may vary from specimen to specimen, but the angles between them remain constant because of the orderly arrangement of ions or atoms throughout the crystal. Some elements or compounds may develop into more than one crystal form (e.g., carbon as graphite and diamond).

To simplify construction of the basic crystal systems, a solid piece of wood was cut on a table saw. This eliminates the construction difficulty of attempting to fasten styrofoam balls on sticks at different angles. The solid wood models have proved more durable for classroom use.

Photo 26

CRYSTAL SYSTEMS MODELS DIAGRAM 26

THESE MODELS WERE MADE OF 2"STOCK. CHARACTERISTICS OF EACH
WERE PRINTED ON MODELS WITH FINE-POINT MARKER.

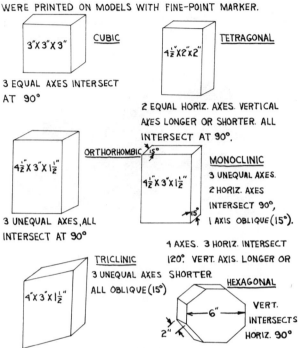

CUBIC

3"X 3"X 3"

3 EQUAL AXES INTERSECT
AT 90°

TETRAGONAL

1½"X 2"X 2"

2 EQUAL HORIZ. AXES. VERTICAL
AXES LONGER OR SHORTER. ALL
INTERSECT AT 90°.

ORTHORHOMBIC

4½"X 3"X 1½"

3 UNEQUAL AXES, ALL
INTERSECT AT 90°

MONOCLINIC

4½"X 3"X 1½"

3 UNEQUAL AXES.
2 HORIZ. AXES
INTERSECT 90°,
1 AXIS OBLIQUE (15°).

TRICLINIC

4"X 3"X 1½"

3 UNEQUAL AXES
ALL OBLIQUE (15°)

4 AXES. 3 HORIZ. INTERSECT
120°. VERT. AXIS. LONGER OR
SHORTER.

HEXAGONAL

6"

2"

VERT.
INTERSECTS
HORIZ. 90°

FAULT MODEL

A fracture in the earth's crust along which movement has occurred is known as a fault. A basis for classification of faults is the relative movement of rock masses on opposite sides of the fault. The sections separated by a fault are named as they were by miners who encountered faults underground. The block that hangs overhead is called the "hanging wall" and the block walked on is known as the "foot wall."

Normal faults—the hanging wall moves downward in relation to the foot wall.
Thrust fault—hanging wall moves upward.
Strike—slip fault—horizontal movement along fault.

Hinge fault—displacement ends at a point away from opening.

It is suggested in constructing the model that the size be approximately 3″ x 20″ x 7″. If enamel paints are used the rock symbols can be identified by symbols, using a fine-point marker.

Photo 27

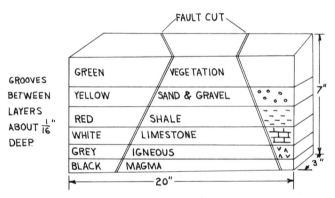

FAULT MODEL   DIAGRAM 27

GROOVES
BETWEEN
LAYERS
ABOUT $\frac{1}{16}$″
DEEP

GREEN	VEGETATION	
YELLOW	SAND & GRAVEL	
RED	SHALE	
WHITE	LIMESTONE	
GREY	IGNEOUS	
BLACK	MAGMA	

FAULT CUT

7″

3″

20″

CUT GROOVES TO SEPARATE LAYERS ON TABLE SAW BEFORE
FINAL FAULT CUTS ARE MADE (CUT GROOVES ALL
AROUND BLOCK).
USE ENAMEL PAINTS FOR LAYERS & IDENTIFY ROCK
LAYERS WITH CORRECT SYMBOLS USING PERMANENT
FINE-POINT MARKER AFTER PAINT HAS DRIED
THOROUGHLY.
SIZE MAY BE VARIED.

SPECIFIC GRAVITY

The number of times a substance is as heavy as an equal volume of water is called its specific gravity. (Example—1 cubic centimeter of water weighs 1 gram, 1 cubic centimeter of gold weighs 19.3 grams—therefore the specific gravity of gold is 19.3). The specific gravity of any substance can be found from the following formula:

$$S.G. = \frac{\text{Weight of a substance}}{\text{Weight of equal volume of water}}$$

Because almost all rocks are solids that sink, they will displace a volume of water equal to their own volume. Therefore we can say that the specific gravity of a sinking body can be found by the following formula:

$$S.G. = \frac{\text{Weight of solid}}{\text{Weight of displaced water}}$$

In our experiment, the sample is weighed in air in the wire basket. (The weight of the basket must be deducted.) The sample is immersed in water by lifting the plastic bucket, and an apparent loss in weight is recorded. By subtracting the weight recorded while the sample was submerged in water from the weight in air, we find the weight of the displaced water. By dividing the weight of the solid by the weight of the displaced water we arrive at S.G.

It is suggested that students bring in available samples because prolonged immersion in water adds to the weight of the sample and affects the computations.

In the same illustration are directions for constructing inexpensive but very practical ringstands.

Photo 28

SPECIFIC GRAVITY   DIAGRAM 28

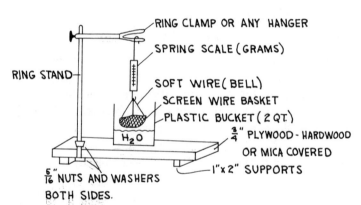

RING CLAMP OR ANY HANGER

SPRING SCALE (GRAMS)

RING STAND

SOFT WIRE (BELL)

SCREEN WIRE BASKET

PLASTIC BUCKET (2 QT.)

$\frac{3}{4}$" PLYWOOD - HARDWOOD

OR MICA COVERED

H_2O

1"x 2" SUPPORTS

$\frac{5}{16}$" NUTS AND WASHERS
BOTH SIDES.

SPECIFIC GRAVITY EXP.

WEIGH SAMPLE IN WIRE BASKET. DEDUCT WEIGHT OF
WIRE BASKET.

RAISE BUCKET TO SUBMERGE SAMPLE.

COMPUTE SPECIFIC GRAVITY.

RING STAND

BASE 8"X 12"X $\frac{3}{4}$", MICA OR HARDWOOD COVERED.

SUPPORT $\frac{5}{16}$" ROD, THREADED 1$\frac{3}{4}$" FROM BOTTOM.

2 NUTS & 2 WASHERS (ALUM. ROD PREFERRED).

FOLDED MOUNTAINS MODEL

The Rockies, Appalachians, Alps, and Himalayas are some examples of the world's folded mountain ranges. These complex structures generally result where rock strata have been subjected to pressures beyond their elastic limit and may yield slowly by bending or folding into symmetrical folds with alternating crests and troughs. The crests are called "anticlines" and the troughs "synclines."

Geologists once believed that folding was caused entirely by horizontal pressure or compression, but experiments have shown that many kinds of folds may occur in layered material around a rising mass as it pushes upward.

In addition to illustrating folded rock layers, the model can illustrate the formation resulting from weathering and erosion by tacking a piece of paper across the anticline section of the fold.

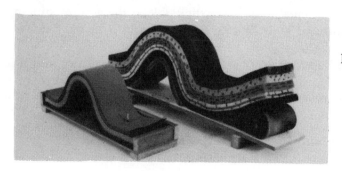

Photo 29

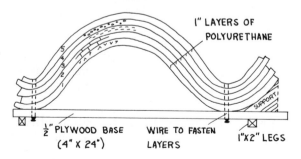

FOLDED MOUNTAINS MODEL DIAGRAM 29

1" LAYERS OF POLYURETHANE

SUPPORT

½" PLYWOOD BASE (4" X 24")

WIRE TO FASTEN LAYERS

1"X2" LEGS

CONSTRUCTION:
SPRAY-PAINT EDGES OF LAYERS TO REPRESENT ROCK
LAYERS.
IDENTIFY LAYERS WITH SYMBOLS. USE MAGIC MARKER.
FASTEN LAYERS TO BASE WITH WIRE. (PASS WIRE
THROUGH LAYERS).
SIZE MAY VARY.
KEY
   1- BASALT - GREY - ∨∧⋗
   2- LIMESTONE - WHITE - ⊥⊥⊤⊥
   3- SHALE - RED - ‾⁻‾⁻‾
   4- SAND & GRAVEL - YELLOW - °₀°∘°
   5- VEGETATION - GREEN

FLAME TESTS

To make simple flame tests, a nichrome wire (platinum if available) with a small loop on the end should be used. The wire should be fastened to a dowel stick. Clean the wire by dipping it in concentrated hydrochloric acid and hold it in the flame until there is no color.

The substance to be tested should be ground up into a fine powder. Dip the wire loop in the acid and touch some of the powdered mineral with the moistened loop. Hold the loop in the flame and note the color.

Strontium	—	Violet
Lithium	—	Bright Red
Calcium	—	Orange-red
Sodium	—	Yellow-orange
Barium	—	Yellow-green
Copper	—	Green
Potassium	—	Violet

It is suggested that an individual wire loop be made for each chemical to be tested. Chemical compounds may be obtained from the laboratory to illustrate the flame produced by different minerals.

The flame test is a method used to help identify minerals by the coloration of the flame in which their powder is placed.

Photo 30

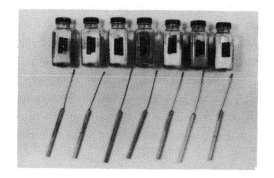

FLAME TESTS FOR MINERALS DIAGRAM 30

COMPOUNDS OF THE FOLLOWING ELEMENTS

SODIUM	LITHIUM	POTASSIUM	CALCIUM	$CuSO_4$	$CuCl$
(YELLOW)	(CRIMSON)	(VIOLET)	(ORANGE)	(GREEN)	(BLUE)

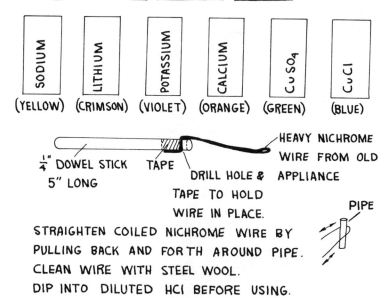

$\frac{1}{4}"$ DOWEL STICK TAPE HEAVY NICHROME WIRE FROM OLD APPLIANCE
5" LONG

DRILL HOLE & TAPE TO HOLD WIRE IN PLACE.

PIPE

STRAIGHTEN COILED NICHROME WIRE BY
PULLING BACK AND FORTH AROUND PIPE.
CLEAN WIRE WITH STEEL WOOL.
DIP INTO DILUTED HCl BEFORE USING.

IT IS SUGGESTED TO MAKE INDIVIDUAL WIRES FOR
EACH MINERAL USED TO OBTAIN THE SAME COLOR.
LABEL EACH STICK WITH FINE-POINT MARKER.

RAINMAKER

The cycle of evaporation, condensation, and precipitation can be demonstrated by the Rainmaker. The heat source supplies the energy for the evaporation of the water. The water vapor rises in the jar and comes in contact with the cold copper tubing, through which cold water flows continuously. The change from invisible water vapor to visible water drops (condensation) is observable on the copper tubing. As condensation continues, the water droplets increase in size and drop back into the boiling liquid in the jar.

It is suggested that a small, bent wire be placed over the top edge of the jar. This permits excessive pressure to escape between the top of the jar and the metal lid. A Pyrex jar must be used for the experiment.

Photo 31

RAINMAKER   DIAGRAM 31

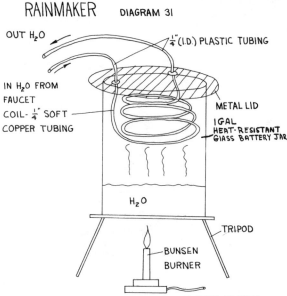

HOT PLATE CAN BE SUBSTITUTED FOR BUNSEN BURNER
AND TRIPOD.
HEATED WATER EVAPORATES AND VAPOR CONDENSES ON
WATER-COOLED TUBING, FORMING WATER DROPLETS
WHICH FALL BACK INTO H_2O.

CENTRIFUGAL HOOP

Careful measurements show that the weight of an object is not exactly the same all over the earth. An object weighs less at the equator than it does at the poles. This means that the object must be nearer the earth's center at the poles than at the equator. The earth is not a perfect sphere but is flattened at the poles and bulges at the equator.

The centrifugal hoop attempts to prove a hypothesis that the earth's rotation on its axis produces a resulting centrifugal force, which causes the bulge at the equator and flattening at the poles.

It must be cautioned that the hoop must be held in place by the palm of one hand while the other hand controls the rotating speed. As the speed is increased, the flattening effect of the hoop is easily visible. A corresponding notch must be filed in the hoop rod to fit the mixer drive rod.

Photo 32

CENTRIFUGAL LOOP DEMONSTRATION
DIAGRAM 32

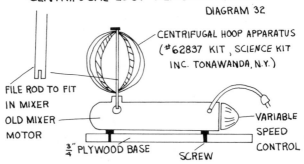

CENTRIFUGAL HOOP APPARATUS
(#62837 KIT, SCIENCE KIT INC. TONAWANDA, N.Y.)

FILE ROD TO FIT
IN MIXER
OLD MIXER
MOTOR

VARIABLE
SPEED
CONTROL

$\frac{3}{4}$" PLYWOOD BASE   SCREW

PROCEDURE:
OBTAIN OLD MIXER MOTOR AND MOUNT UPSIDE DOWN
ON WOOD BASE.
FILE NOTCH IN CENTRIFUGAL HOOP APPARATUS ROD
TO FIT INTO MIXER.
PLACE HAND ON TOP OF ROD TO KEEP ROD FROM
BECOMING DISENGAGED FROM SLOT.
VARY SPEEDS.
(DEMONSTRATES EFFECT OF CENTRIFUGAL FORCE ON
A ROTATING MASS--EARTH'S BULGE AT EQUATOR).

SOIL HORIZONS

Soil is a natural surface material that supports plant life. Soils exhibit certain properties that are determined by climate and living organisms operating over periods of time on earth materials and on landscapes of varying relief. A natural or artificial exposure of a soil reveals a series of zones, each different from the one above. Each zone is called a horizon. The three major soil horizons are described below:

A Horizon—uppermost zone into which we plant seeds; characterized by vegetation.

B Horizon—lies directly below A Horizon and contains clay-like materials and iron oxides delivered by water that has percolated down.

C Horizon—consists of partially disintegrated and decomposed rock material.

Each community has its own soil characteristics. The model provides an idea for investigating soil horizons at any location. The soils can be collected in glass jars or clear plastic containers for observation, labeling, and comparison. A larger collecting container makes the soil easily visible for display.

Photo 33

SOIL HORIZONS DIAGRAM 33

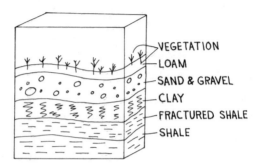

VEGETATION
LOAM
SAND & GRAVEL
CLAY
FRACTURED SHALE
SHALE

CONSTRUCT BOX WITH TV GLASS FRONT FASTENED TO
BOX (AQUARIUM SATISFACTORY).
COLLECT AND IDENTIFY LOCAL HORIZON SAMPLES.
PLACE THIN PLASTIC SHEET BETWEEN LAYERS.
IDENTIFY LAYERS ON CONTAINER.

PROFILE MODELS

The profile map represents both vertical and horizontal dimensions of a cross-section of the earth's surface across a given line. By constructing profile models, a student can illustrate the dimension of depth and thus portray more effectively a section of land.

This activity lends itself to a wide variety of substitution of materials, from pieces of wood to plaster of paris. Unlimited land forms can be constructed by constructing one layer at a time, painting and labeling it, and finally assembling the model. It is suggested that models of local areas be constructed. The local elevations (contour lines) can be projected from a 7.5 min. quadrangle geological map on a large piece of paper, and then the pieces can be constructed and assembled.

Photo 34

PROFILE MODELS DIAGRAM 34

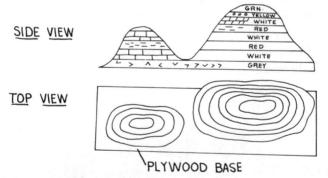

USE WHITE PINE SCRAPS (OR OTHER LIGHT WOOD)
FOR INDIVIDUAL LAYERS.
SPRAY-PAINT EDGES AND PART OF SURFACE NEAR
EDGES BEFORE STACKING.
MARK SYMBOLS WITH FINE, PERMANENT MARKER.
SIZE MAY BE VARIED.
ORDER OF LAYERS MAY BE VARIED TO CORRESPOND
TO LOCAL GEOLOGY.

MINERAL IDENTIFICATION

A mineral is a naturally occurring inorganic substance with a definite chemical composition and a definite orderly arrangement of its elements. Although more than 2000 minerals are known, we usually need more than one of their physical properties for identification in addition to chemical properties.

In the mineral identification activity, any substitute containers will serve the purpose. Listed below are physical and chemical characteristics and suggested mineral samples that could be combined to introduce a lesson in mineral identification. Many substitutions are possible.

CHARACTERISTICS		MINERAL
1. Crystal form	—	Quartz
2. Hardness	—	Talc
3. Specific Gravity	—	Basalt
4. Cleavage	—	Feldspar
5. Color	—	Olivine
6. Streak	—	Hematite
7. Luster	—	Galena
8. Fracture	—	Obsidian
9. Chemical	—	Calcite

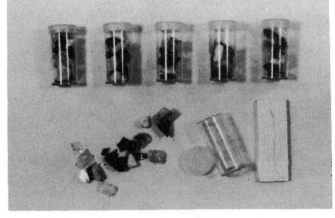

Photo 35

INTRODUCTION to MINERAL IDENTIFICATION
DIAGRAM 35

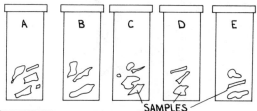

OBJECTIVE:

TO INTRODUCE METHODS OF IDENTIFYING MINERALS
(LUSTER, STREAK, FRACTURE, XLS, ETC.)

MAKE 10 SETS USING PLASTIC CONTAINERS (OR BABY
FOOD JARS) AND PLACE INSIDE SMALL SAMPLES OF
QUARTZ, MICA, GALENA, TALC AND OTHER AVAILABLE
SMALL SAMPLES.

PLACE 1 JAR PER GROUP AND HAVE THEM IDENTIFY
MINERAL AND ITS CHARACTERISTICS.

LIST CHARACTERISTICS ON CHALKBOARD OR
PROVIDE WORKSHEET.

COLLECTION COULD BE USED FOR INDIVIDUAL
OR GROUP WORK.

CLOUD MAKER

Clouds consist of very small water particles. As a warm current of air rises from the earth, it expands and cools. When it rises to a height where the dew point is reached, condensation begins and clouds are formed.

To produce a cloud with the model, place about a pint of warm water in a gallon jug. Make the walls of the jug wet by swirling the water around. Drop a lighted match or blow smoke into the jar. Replace the stopper and pump air into the jug with the hand jump. (Care should be taken to avoid excessive air pressure because the jug may not withstand high internal pressure.) Suddenly remove the stopper and a fog is produced as the temperature and pressure is reduced. The smoke acts as the condensation nuclei.

Photo 36

CLOUD MAKER   DIAGRAM 36

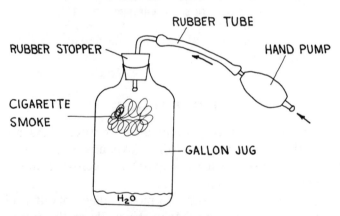

SWIRL TO WET INSIDE OF JUG.
BLOW SMOKE INTO BOTTLE OR DROP LIGHTED MATCH TO
SUPPLY CONDENSATION NUCLEI.
INCREASE PRESSURE INSIDE JUG WITH HAND PUMP.
(A BICYCLE PUMP WILL DO, BUT CARE MUST BE
 TAKEN BECAUSE TOO MUCH PRESSURE WILL BREAK JUG)
DECREASE PRESSURE BY RELEASING STOPPER AND
A CLOUD WILL APPEAR INSIDE JUG.

SEDIMENTATION CHAMBER

The process by which rock-forming material is laid down is called deposition or sedimentation. The material that is deposited is usually in the form of gravel, sand, silt, and clay derived from weathering and erosion of a land area. Its movement is usually from a higher area to a lower area, and it is usually transported by water. The deposition occurs when water no longer has enough energy to carry the material further.

The construction of the sedimentation chamber can be varied in many ways, but it is essential that a transparent side be available for viewing the sedimentation process.

The sedimentation chamber provides an activity where the students can observe the processes of the settling of sediments and beach development. The sediments are introduced to the chamber by flushing with running water down an inclined trough.

The water that enters the chamber is allowed to exit through a pipe on the opposite end. If it is desired to increase the level of deposits, the lower exit can be stoppered and a higher exit can be installed.

It is suggested that a variety of colored sands be used as sediments. The sands could be sprayed after they are dried thoroughly. Fine-grained fish tank gravel works satisfactorily.

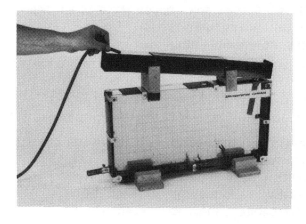

Photo 37

SEDIMENTATION CHAMBER   DIAGRAM 37

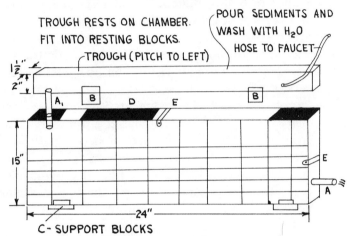

TROUGH RESTS ON CHAMBER.
FIT INTO RESTING BLOCKS.
TROUGH (PITCH TO LEFT)

POUR SEDIMENTS AND
WASH WITH H_2O
HOSE TO FAUCET

$1\frac{1}{2}$"

2"

A_1 B   D   E   B

15"

E

A

24"

C- SUPPORT BLOCKS

A- PLASTIC OVERFLOW TUBE ($\frac{3}{4}$" I.D.) DRILL HOLE 3"
FROM BOTTOM OF CHAMBER AND CEMENT
BEFORE CHAMBER IS ASSEMBLED.

A_1 - INPUT TUBE ($\frac{3}{4}$" I.D.) DRILL HOLE $1\frac{1}{2}$" FROM END
OF TROUGH AND CEMENT TUBE IN PLACE. DRILL
CORRESPONDING HOLE IN REINFORCING PIECE TO
RECEIVE INPUT TUBE.

B- RESTING BLOCKS FOR TROUGH. MAKE TO FIT OVER
CHAMBER AND TO HOLD TROUGH. (⊓) MAKE 2
SIZES TO PROVIDE PITCH FOR H_2O FLOW.

C - SUPPORT BLOCKS (⊔) TO SERVE AS BASE.
BOTH SAME SIZE.

D- SHADED AREAS ARE REINFORCING PIECES.

E- REINFORCE WITH ALUMINUM STRAPS IF NECESSARY.

ALL PLASTIC MATERIALS ($\frac{1}{4}$" THICK) CUT TO SIZE
AND HELD TOGETHER WITH MASKING TAPE. CEMENT
WITH QUICK-ACTING PLASTIC CEMENT. (I USED
A HYPODERMIC NEEDLE WITH CADO SC-94
CEMENT) (CADILLAC PLASTICS, LINDEN, N.J.).

STREAM TABLE

The water that flows in a river transports debris, erodes the river channel, and deposits sediments. The material that a stream transports is picked up directly from its own channel. As soon as the velocity of the stream decreases significantly, it begins to deposit its suspended load.

The opportunity to study surface land forms and erosional changes can be accomplished with the stream table. Meandering streams, deltas, dams, and erosion by rivers can be simulated. A rainfall simulator can be easily constructed from sheet metal.

A circulating pump keeps the water flow continuous but a siphon can be used to empty the lower end and water can be introduced at the upper end manually. The pitch of the table can be changed by lifting the stream table in its frame holder and inserting wood blocks.

It is suggested that a mixture of fine and coarse sand be used with various-sized rocks to provide realistic demonstrations of water flow.

The wave generator illustrated in the photograph consists of a slow-speed motor and a flat piece of aluminum connected to a rod and mounted on a cam. The generator is placed in the stream table so that the flat aluminum metal plunges to a depth of about ½" on its downstroke. After about 15 minutes of operation, a good demonstration of beach erosion by wave motion is evident.

(Ref. *Circulating Pump*—Edmund Scientific, Barrington, N.J.)

Photo 38

STREAM TABLE   DIAGRAM 38

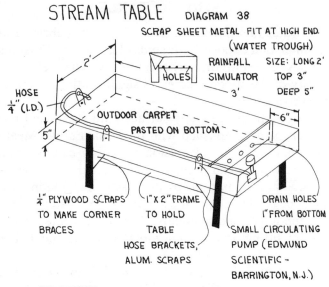

SCRAP SHEET METAL FIT AT HIGH END.
(WATER TROUGH)
RAINFALL   SIZE: LONG 2'
SIMULATOR   TOP 3"
DEEP 5"

2'

HOSE
$\frac{1}{4}$" (I.D.)

3'

OUTDOOR CARPET
PASTED ON BOTTOM

6"

HOLES

5"

$\frac{1}{4}$" PLYWOOD SCRAPS
TO MAKE CORNER
BRACES

1" X 2" FRAME
TO HOLD
TABLE

DRAIN HOLES
1" FROM BOTTOM

HOSE BRACKETS,
ALUM. SCRAPS

SMALL CIRCULATING
PUMP (EDMUND
SCIENTIFIC –
BARRINGTON, N.J.)

PROCEDURE:

1. SHEET METAL 4'6" x 3' (HEAVY GAUGE) CUT OUT
   CORNERS TO MAKE BOX. SOLDER CORNERS.
2. SCRAP SHEET METAL DIVIDER. 6" FROM LOWER
   END WITH DRAIN HOLES APPROX. 1" FROM
   BOTTOM SOLDER TO BOX.
3. SCRAP SHEETMETAL TO MAKE RAINFALL
   SIMULATOR.
4. MAKE FRAME TO ACCEPT TABLE WITH
   10° ELEVATION.
5. HOSE $\frac{1}{4}$" (I.D.) APPROX. 5'.
6. REINFORCE CORNERS WITH PLYWOOD SCRAPS.
7. WASH SAND BEFORE USING TO AVOID
   CLOGGING PUMP.

GEYSER

Boiling hot springs that erupt from time to time as gushers
of hot water and steam are called geysers. A geyser eruption can
be compared to an explosion of a pressure cooker. Ground water,
under pressure of the water above, is "superheated" to a tempera-

ture above the water's normal boiling point. The superheated water explodes into steam, blowing out the water above it in the form of a geyser eruption.

The model illustrated has worked with excellent results. The substitutions used allow for easy storage (folding legs). Drill a ⅜-inch hole in a copper strip one inch in diameter, and solder it to the ⅜-inch copper tubbing about one inch from the end that is fitted into the can. Then solder the copper strip (with tubing attached) to the can. This prevents molten solder from seeping into the can. Be sure to keep the seam of the can on the "up" side when constructing the "boiler."

Photo 39

Make the following checks before operation:

1. Be sure the system is complete with hoses, copper tubing and can. Blow through either opening to check for open passage.
2. Fill the system with water and force water through system.
3. Refill the system to replace water that is lost.

The first eruption is usually incomplete because the system is not thoroughly heated.

(Ref.—*Geology & Earth Sciences Sourcebook,* Robert L. Heller, Editor. © 1962 by Holt, Rinehart, & Winston, Inc., p. 79.)

WORKING MODEL GEYSER   DIAGRAM 39

(x) SCRAPS 1"X 2" TO BUILD
GEYSER ELEVATION

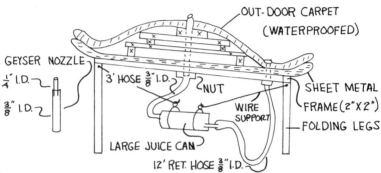

OUT-DOOR CARPET
(WATERPROOFED)

GEYSER NOZZLE
$\frac{1}{4}$" I.D.

$\frac{3}{8}$" I.D.

3' HOSE $\frac{3}{8}$" I.D.

NUT

WIRE SUPPORT

SHEET METAL
FRAME (2"X 2")

FOLDING LEGS

LARGE JUICE CAN

12' RET. HOSE $\frac{3}{8}$" I.D.

SUGGESTED TO USE $\frac{3}{8}$" (I.D.) RUBBER TUBING.

SUPPORT OUTPUT RUBBER HOSE TO MAKE CONTINUOUS UPWARD
DIRECTION OF FLOW.

DO NOT REAM FINAL CUT IN $\frac{1}{4}$" C.T. FOR GEYSER NOZZLE.

REAM $\frac{1}{4}$" C.T. END THAT FITS INTO $\frac{3}{8}$" C.T.

RETURN

12 GAUGE WIRE

OUTLET
TUBE

6" C.T.
SOLDER
TO CAN

8" C.T. SOLDER
TO CAN

($\frac{3}{8}$" COPPER TUBE) (C.T.)

USE 2 PROPANE OR BUNSEN
BURNERS. SYSTEM MUST
BE FILLED WITH H_2O AND
FULLY HEATED FOR SUCCESS-
FUL OPERATION. REFILL
LOST H_2O.

chapter 5

Activities with
Electrical Projects

Although it may sound strange, electrical energy by itself is practically useless until it is converted to some other form of energy such as light, heat, mechanical or sound.

The fundamentals of electricity are based upon magnetism, and magnetism is based upon the structure and behavior of the atom. The arrangement of groups of atoms in ferromagnetic materials determines a magnet's characteristics. The effects of magnetism are felt in all the electrical devices we have available at our command.

The electrical energy supplied to us by the power companies is converted into the different forms of energy which we use. In reality, we are paying for the work done by the electrical energy supplied to us. The energy used is measured by a meter installed in homes by power companies. The difference between successive readings tells us the amount of energy consumed and the resulting cost to the consumer.

This chapter focuses on a number of inexpensive projects that illustrate basic concepts in electricity. Included in the chapter are projects using batteries and others using power available at the outlet. It must be remembered that used properly, electricity is safe. Do not take chances with electrical devices if you do not understand them. Handled carelessly, it is dangerous. The purpose here is to develop a respect for its capacity and an understanding of its dangers.

ELECTRICAL QUIZZER

The electrical quizzer provides an opportunity to construct an inexpensive and safe electrical device that has application in other subject areas. The quizzer consists of two push buttons, a bell, a miniature light socket and bulb, and a 1.5 volt dry cell.

Illustrated in the diagram are the connections at the terminals of the push buttons which permit individual operation by two students. A dry cell is connected in series with a bell to act as a sounder. As an additional feature, a miniature light bulb is connected parallel with the bell. All the parts are mounted on a wood base, but it is suggested that the push buttons be separated to provide comfortable operation by two students.

The quizzer can be used to stimulate class interest in reviewing subject matter written in question and answer form as a quiz game. Any subject area is adaptable to the quiz board. It is further suggested that two quizzers be constructed to involve four students simultaneously. In addition, a different type of sounder (such as a buzzer) and colored light bulbs help to identify the first response to questions during any quiz.

The quiz game can easily be written by writing matching questions and answers. Short phrases and one word answers work very well. In math, flash cards are easily adapted.

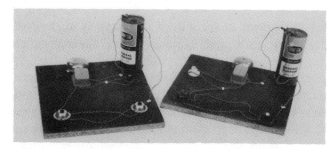

Photo 40

ELECTRICAL QUIZZER DIAGRAM 40

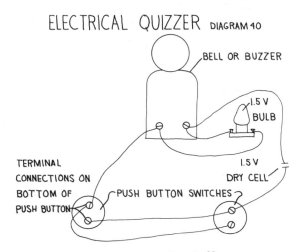

BELL OR BUZZER

1.5 V BULB

TERMINAL CONNECTIONS ON BOTTOM OF PUSH BUTTON

PUSH BUTTON SWITCHES

1.5 V DRY CELL

FASTEN PARTS ON BASE 12" X 12" x ¾" PLYWOOD.
MAKE TWO SETS. THIS PERMITS 2 STUDENTS TO
COMPETE AGAINST 2 OTHER STUDENTS.
SUGGEST COLORED BULBS, BUZZER OR BELL.
LIGHT AND BUZZER CAN BE ACTIVATED BY
ANY BUTTON.
USE FOR SUBJECT MATTER, FLASH CARDS, ETC.

REPULSION COIL

When a conductor forming part of a closed circuit is moved through a magnetic field, a current starts to flow in it. Currents produced in this way are said to be "induced" currents. The direction of the flow of induced current can be reversed if the direction of the movement of the wire is reversed. A current that reverses its direction again and again is called alternating current.

With the repulsion coil we are able to understand Lenz's law, which states that an induced current flows in the opposite direction to that in the primary coil. As a magnetic field is produced in each coil, a repulsion of magnetic fields occurs. The induced current occurs in the aluminum ring, which is repulsed by the primary coil, and the ring is thrown into the air.

The repulsion coil consists of a plastic tube into which is placed a laminated core. The core is bolted to the base by a "U" bolt. A 4″ high primary coil is wound on the tube at the base. The coil consists of 400 turns of #16 enameled wire. Plastic washers made from floor tiles are placed at the top and bottom of the coil. The wire leads from the coil are passed into the base and connected to an AC line plug. A push button is connected in series with the line voltage and is mounted on the top of the base support.

An aluminum ring (2¼″ [id] x 1¾″) is suspended on the magnetic field produced by the primary coil. When the repulsion force equals the pull of gravity, the ring will float on the magnetic field. When the ring is resting on the coil, maximum current is developed in the ring. The reaction between the strong field in the ring and that of the main coil is responsible for the repulsion effect. Keep the push button depressed for short periods of time to prevent overheating of the primary coil.

The transformer effect can be demonstrated by placing a portable coil (22 turns of #16 wire), with a 6 volt lamp connected to the ends of the coil, over the core. As the coil is moved closer to the core, the light in the bulb increases until it burns at maximum near the main coil. An electric bell can be connected to another coil (11 turns of #16 wire) and the same effect can be noticed. Current is induced in the secondary coils as is done in a transformer.

Photo 41

REPULSION COIL   DIAGRAM 41

SECONDARY LIGHT COIL

22 T #16 WIRE
6 V AUTO BULB

PLASTIC TUBE
2"(O.D.) 15" LENGTH

PLASTIC WASHERS MADE
FROM PLASTIC FLOOR
TILE

COIL - 400 TURNS   4"
#16 ENAMELED WIRE
WASHER

SECONDARY BELL COIL

11 T #16 WIRE, 3 V BELL

$1\frac{1}{2}$" { ALUMINUM PIPE
$1\frac{1}{2}$" TO FIT LOOSELY
OVER PLASTIC PIPE
CORE- STRAP IRON, SPRAY-
PAINT ALL SIDES AND
RIVET TOGETHER INSIDE
PLASTIC TUBE.
U-BOLT (FASTENS CORE)
HEAVY PUSH BUTTON
SWITCH
(NORMALLY OPEN)

6"

12"

BASE - $\frac{1}{2}$" PLYWOOD

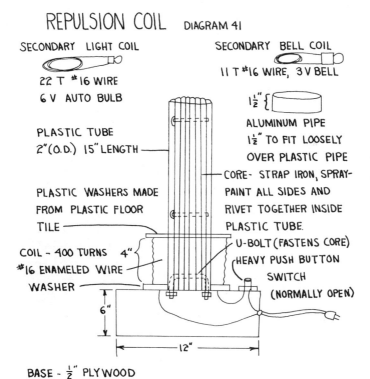

OVERLOAD DEMONSTRATION

When current flows through a circuit, the electric wires are constantly being heated by the current flowing through them. If too much current is allowed to flow through the circuit, the wires may burn their insulation and start a fire. When too many devices are connected to one outlet, the circuit is said to be "overloaded." To prevent overloading, fuses or circuit breakers are inserted in circuits as protecting devices. The fuse is constructed with a fine wire with a low melting point so that it melts when the current becomes too great, stopping the flow of current. A circuit breaker "trips" and opens the circuit when dangerous conditions are reached.

In the demonstration, a resistance outlet is provided where many electrical devices can be connected. As each resistance (appliance or tool) is turned on, the additional current being used is recorded by the ammeter. When the rate of current approaches the capacity of the circuit breaker (or the fuse) the circuit will be opened, no current will flow, and the ammeter should return to zero.

A fuse receptacle could be substituted for the circuit breaker. Care should be taken that the value of the circuit breaker or fuse be less than the line (input) value.

Photo 42

RESISTANCE AND OVERLOAD DEMONSTRATION
DIAGRAM 42

CONNECT VOLTMETER IN PARALLEL WITH POWER INPUT.
CONNECT AMMETER, RESISTANCE OUTLET, CIRCUIT BREAKER
AND SWITCH IN SERIES WITH POWER INPUT.
ADD RESISTANCES AND OBSERVE VOLTAGE AND
CURRENT READINGS ON METER.
OVERLOAD CIRCUIT AND CIRCUIT BREAKER OPENS
CIRCUIT.
USE #16 INSULATED WIRE.
A LAMP BASE CAN BE SUBSTITUTED FOR THE
CIRCUIT BREAKER AND FUSES USED.

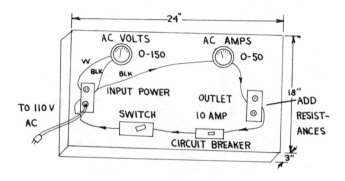

MAGNETS

Over 2000 years ago, it was discovered that an iron ore called magnetite is able to attract and hold small bits of iron. Because magnetite is already magnetized when found in nature, it is called a natural magnet. Today we know that a magnet can attract not only pieces of iron, but certain other metals such as nickel and cobalt. Magnetism is an invisible force that has the ability to attract magnetic substances.

If a magnet is sprinkled with iron filings, we notice that these filings are not attracted uniformly to the whole surface, but rather seem to cluster at either end of the magnet. It appears that the magnetism is concentrated at two ends of the magnet. We call the two ends of the magnet poles, and further experimentation confirms the fact that like poles repel and unlike poles attract each other.

The simple model illustrates two circular magnets repelling each other. Magnetic lines of force can be clearly demonstrated by placing a magnet on an overhead projector, covering the magnet with a plate of glass or heavy plastic, and sprinkling iron filings over the surface. The projection illustrates the concentration of iron filings at the poles and the paths taken by the lines of force.

Many variations of lines of force can be projected on the screen. A combination of bar, horseshoe, and circular magnets can be projected at the same time to illustrate repulsion and attraction of magnetic poles. The circular magnets present an interesting investigation to determine the location of the poles.

Photo 43

MAGNETS   DIAGRAM 43

— CARDBOARD OR PLASTIC TUBE

CIRCULAR MAGNETS

BASE

GROOVES CUT INTO BASE (GLUE)

BY REVERSING MAGNETS, REPULSION AND
ATTRACTION CAN BE ILLUSTRATED.
PAINT MAGNETS DIFFERENT COLORS.
SIZE OF TUBE DEPENDS UPON SIZE OF
CIRCULAR MAGNETS.

HIGH-VOLTAGE TRAVELING ARC

A device that is used to change voltages of alternating current is the transformer. It consists of a primary coil and a secondary coil wound on a soft iron core. The coils are insulated from each other. When alternating current is passed through the primary coil, it sets up an alternating magnetic field that sweeps back and forth across the secondary coil. An alternating electromotive force is induced in the secondary coil. The magnitude of the secondary coil depends upon the number of turns in the secondary coil and the electromotive force applied to the primary.

The high-voltage traveling arc illustrated was constructed from a 7500 volt (secondary) sign transformer. It is basically a step-up transformer with a 115 volt primary winding. The two secondary leads are fastened to insulating posts, and two aluminum rods (18″ in length) are fastened to the insulating posts. The gap at the bottom of the rods is approximately ⅛″ and the top gap is about 1 inch between the rods. The rods must be free from rough edges, because these may act as discharge points and prevent the arc from traveling up the rod. Experimentation may be necessary to find good starting and terminal gaps between the aluminum rods or substitutions. Always disconnect the transformer from the line voltage when working on the equipment.

In addition to illustrating the concept of a transformer, the traveling arc makes a good exhibit to draw attention. When the switch is turned on, a flaming arc jumps between the wires at the short gap above the insulators. Immediately it starts rising to the top, getting longer as the distance between the rods increases. As soon as one arc is extinguished, another one starts. The process continues as long as the switch is closed.

The flaming arc rises because the air is heated in the vicinity of the arc, and the heated air rises and pulls the arc up with it.

The heavy plastic is placed around the transformer for protection against accidental contact.

Other transformers (oil burner) are adaptable to the demonstration model provided the rating is between 7500 and 10,000 volts. *Take extreme caution in working with such transformers because the charge can be very dangerous.*

THIS DEMONSTRATION SHOULD BE DONE ONLY BY THE TEACHER!!

Photo 44

HIGH VOLTAGE TRAVELING ARC DIAGRAM 44

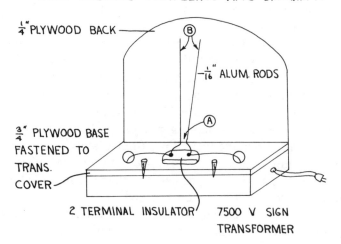

$\frac{1}{4}$" PLYWOOD BACK

Ⓑ

$-\frac{1}{16}$" ALUM. RODS

Ⓐ

$\frac{3}{4}$" PLYWOOD BASE FASTENED TO TRANS. COVER

2 TERMINAL INSULATOR   7500 V SIGN TRANSFORMER

FASTEN INSULATOR TO PLYWOOD BASE.
SET STARTING GAP Ⓐ APPROX. $\frac{1}{8}$"
SET TERMINAL GAP Ⓑ APPROX 1"
STAPLE HEAVY PLASTIC ON $\frac{3}{4}$" PLYWOOD AND $\frac{1}{4}$" PLYWOOD
BACK, ALL AROUND MODEL FOR SAFETY.
USE EXTREME CAUTION! HIGH VOLTAGE PRESENT!
IF ARC DOES NOT TRAVEL UP RODS, DISCONNECT
AND INCREASE STARTING GAP SLIGHTLY.

MAGNETIZER

The molecules of a magnetized substance act as tiny magnets that theoretically line up in an orderly array, with the north pole of one molecule facing the south pole of another molecule. The molecules of a substance that is not magnetized are arranged in a disorderly fashion within the substance so that the magnetic effects of the molecules cancel each other out.

The magnetizer was constructed to remagnetize bar magnets that had lost their magnetism due to careless handling or careless storage. The heart of the magnetizer is a coil of 500 turns wound around a cardboard or plastic tube. The diameter of the tube should be large enough to receive two bar magnets at the same time.

A fuse is constructed from two pieces of #10 wire. A small strip (⅛" wide) of aluminum foil is connected between both wires. When the switch completes the circuit, a surge of current energizes the coil and the lines of force pass through the metal, causing it to become magnetized. The surge of current (AC) burns the fuse, preventing the opposite half of the AC cycle to reverse its path. This would cancel the effects of the first surge of current.

Because of exposed wires at the fuse, care must be taken that students do not accidentally touch the exposed wires. A severe shock is possible. Experimentation can involve variation in construction of the coil, and attempts to pass more than one surge of current through metals placed in the coil.

Photo 45

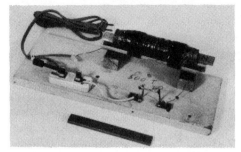

MAGNETIZER   DIAGRAM 45

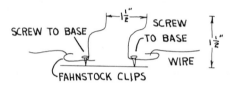

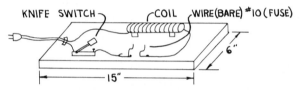

COIL- 500 TURNS #20 ENAMELED WIRE. WRAP ON
     CARDBOARD OR PLASTIC TUBE SIZE 7"x 1"(I.D.)
     MOUNT ON BLOCKS.
CUT PIECE OF ALUM. FOIL AND WRAP AROUND
FUSE WIRE. ($\frac{1}{8}$" DIA.)
INSERT ITEMS TO BE MAGNETIZED INTO TUBE AND
COMPLETE CIRCUIT AT SWITCH. ALUM. FOIL WILL
BURN WITH A 'POP'.
EXCELLENT FOR RENEWING MAGNETISM IN OLD
BAR MAGNETS.

TWO-WAY LIGHT CIRCUIT

A flight of stairs is generally illuminated by a lamp at the top of the stairs. It is designed so that it could be turned off and on at both the bottom and top of the stairs.

In the demonstration model, two single-pole, double-throw switches are inserted in the "hot" lead. A third wire must be connected between the switches. When the lamp is off, throwing either switch to the opposite position causes the lamp to light again. The lamp can be turned off by either switch by throwing the switch to the opposite position. It is suggested that a wire diagram be drawn to help illustrate the paths taken by the current.

The model illustrated is connected to 115 V line voltage. Batteries and bulbs of comparable value (1.5 volt bulb with a 1.5 dry cell) can be substituted for the line voltage. Simple metal switches (2 position) can be substituted for the residential type switches used on the model.

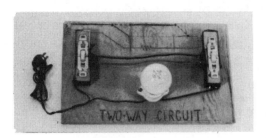

Photo 46

TWO-WAY LIGHT CIRCUIT DIAGRAM 46

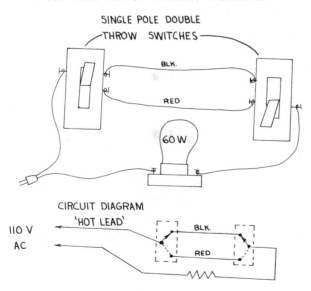

MOUNT PARTS ON 10" X 15" X $\frac{3}{4}$" WOOD BASE.
SUBSTITUTE 1.5 V DRY CELL FOR POWER SOURCE
AND 1.5 V BULB FOR SAFETY.
CIRCUIT CAN BE CONTROLLED BY EITHER SWITCH.
USE #16 INSULATED WIRE.

MAGNETIC PILE DRIVER

If a current is passed through a coil of wire, it behaves like a bar magnet. If the current is turned off, the coil loses its magnetism. An advantage of the electromagnet is that it can be made stronger by adding additional turns of wire to the coil, and by increasing the amount of current flowing through the coil.

The magnetic pile driver is a variation of the electromagnet. It consists of a nonmagnetic hollow core (aluminum tube), a coil of wire wrapped around the aluminum tube, and a movable soft-iron core plunger. When current flows through the coil, the magnetic field tends to pull, or suck, the plunger into the center of the coil. When the current stops, the plunger is pulled out of the coil by either a spring or gravity.

The pile driver operates as a vertically mounted solenoid. When the circuit is completed, the electromagnet "sucks" up a 16 penny nail into the aluminum tube. When the current is stopped, gravity pulls the nail down and it strikes the small aluminum container. This action simulates that of a pile driver.

Photo 47

In the construction, magnet wire (coated) or insulated wire (plastic covered bell wire) must be used. A piece of spring metal can be used as a push button. Experimentation can lead to substitutions for the plunger and size of the coil. The specifications on the construction diagram work satisfactorily.

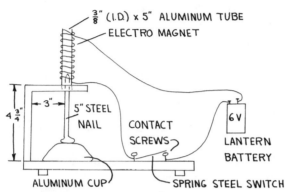

MAGNETIC PILE DRIVER DIAGRAM 47

$\frac{3}{8}''$ (I.D.) x 5" ALUMINUM TUBE

ELECTRO MAGNET

$4\frac{3}{4}''$ — 3" — 5" STEEL NAIL — CONTACT SCREWS — 6 V LANTERN BATTERY

ALUMINUM CUP (OLEOMARGARINE CONTAINER) — SPRING STEEL SWITCH

ELECTROMAGNET - 250 TURNS BELL WIRE ON ALUMINUM TUBE CORE.
REMOVE COATING FROM METAL USED FOR SWITCH.
WHEN SWITCH IS DEPRESSED, NAIL WILL BE 'SUCKED' UP INTO TUBE AND THEN FALL AND HIT ALUMINUM CUP.
BASE SIZE - 5" X 9" X $\frac{3}{4}''$

ELECTRIC BELL

The main parts of an electric bell are the electromagnet, armature made of soft iron, the contact screw, and a gong. Connected in series with the electromagnet is a battery and a push button.

The operation of the bell begins when the push button is depressed; current flows in the electromagnet and causes it to attract the armature. As a result the armature moves away from the contact screw, and the circuit is broken. The electromagnet loses its magnetism and releases the armature, which is pulled back to the contact screw by a spring. Thus the circuit is completed again. Attached to the armature is a hammer which strikes the gong every time the armature is attracted by the electromagnet. As long as the push button is depressed, a continuous ringing sound is produced.

The model consists of a hacksaw blade that acts as the armature. A nut and bolt serve the purpose of a hammer to strike the gong. Experimentation is necessary to obtain the proper gaps between the hacksaw blade and the electromagnets, and between the hammer and the gong.

Care must be taken that the wire be wrapped around the nails in the same direction. It is further suggested to construct the electromagnets with large nuts and bolts. A check should be made to see if the electrical circuit is complete before operation. This can be done if the push bottom is bypassed. If the electromagnet fails to work properly, additional turns of wire could be added to the electromagnet.

Photo 48

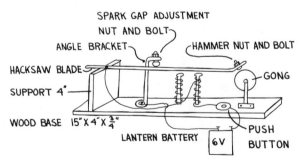

ELECTRIC BELL   DIAGRAM 48

ELECTROMAGNET - 35 TURNS OF BELL WIRE AROUND
2 16 d NAILS. WIND EACH NAIL IN SAME DIRECTION.
SANDPAPER FINISH OFF HACKSAW BLADE AT SPARK
PLUG GAP AND WIRE CONNECTIONS.
ADJUST SPARK GAP SO THAT CIRCUIT IS BROKEN
WHEN ELECTROMAGNET ATTRACTS HACKSAW BLADE.
ADJUST HAMMER TO STRIKE GONG WHEN MAGNET
ATTRACTS HACKSAW BLADE.

CONDUCTORS AND INSULATORS

The current that flows through an electrical device is simply a stream of electrons moving through the wires, in much the same way as water flows through a pipe. A good conductor of electricity allows electrons to move through it freely. All metals are good conductors. Copper is particularly good and is commonly used to make wires for electrical purposes.

A substance through which electrons cannot move freely is an insulator. Rubber, mica, glass, air, and plastics are examples of insulators.

The conductors and insulators model is a collection of different substances mounted on a wood base. A light bulb and battery are connected in series with two soft copper wire leads. The leads are placed in contact at the top and bottom of the substance being tested. If the light bulb lights, the substance is a conductor.

The students should conclude that metals are good conductors of electricity. (Exceptions are nichrome and high resistance wires.) Any number and variety of items for testing are available.

Photo 49

CONDUCTORS AND INSULATORS DIAGRAM 49

1.5 V BULB

ZINC · GLASS · CARBON · ROD · LEATHER · ROPE · TIN · PAPER · FELT

1.5 V DRY CELL

PLASTIC · RUBBER · ASBESTOS · STEEL · COPPER · CORK · ALUMINUM

MOUNT LAMP BASE ON WOOD BASE (12" X 15" X $\frac{3}{4}$").
TACK OR CEMENT TEST SAMPLES ON WOOD BASE.
BARE ENDS OF TEST LEADS (APPROX. 18") AND
TOUCH TOP AND BOTTOM OF SAMPLE.
BULB IS ILLUMINATED WHEN SAMPLE CONDUCTS
CURRENT.

TELEGRAPH

The simple telegraph operates on the principle of starting and stopping the flow of electricity in a wire. Messages are communicated over this circuit by a series of clicks that are interpreted as dots and dashes, which in turn represent letters of the alphabet.

A simple telegraph system consists of two instruments. Each instrument has a key and a sounder. The key is used to open and close the electrical circuit. The sounder consists of an electromagnet, which attracts a piece of soft iron that produces a "click" when the magnet is energized. A click is produced at the moment a current is sent through the sounder and again when the key opens the circuit. If two clicks follow each other in rapid succession, the signal is a dot; if the interval between the clicks is longer, the signal is a dash.

In the illustration, the two models can be connected in series with a 1.5 volt battery. When one operator is sending, the second operator must keep his key depressed. The cabinet hinge acts as the armature which strikes the aluminum rod to produce the clicks. Experimentation may require a rubber band to be attached between the hinge and the base to return the hinge to its rest position quickly. Some metals may have various coatings which act as insulators that prevent the flow of current. These insulators can be easily removed by using a file or sandpaper to permit satisfactory operation of the telegraph.

Photo 50

THE TELEGRAPH DIAGRAM 50

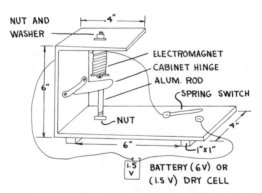

NUT AND WASHER

4"

ELECTROMAGNET
CABINET HINGE
ALUM. ROD
SPRING SWITCH

6"

NUT

4"

6"

1"x1"

1.5 V

BATTERY (6V) OR (1.5 V) DRY CELL

ELECTROMAGNET— 150 TURNS OF BELL WIRE BETWEEN 2 WASHERS ON A 3" BOLT. GAP BETWEEN HINGE AND BOLT APPROX. $\frac{3}{16}$" ADJUST TO OBTAIN BEST RESULTS. HINGE RESTS HORIZONTALLY ON ALUMINUM ROD. WOOD PARTS MADE FROM $\frac{1}{2}$" THICK SCRAPS. CONSTRUCT 2 TELEGRAPHS AND CONNECT IN SERIES WITH BATTERY. (DEPRESS KEY TO RECEIVE).

QUIZBOARD

The construction of the quizboard is based on a simple series circuit which is completed by touching one lead to a question and the second lead to the correct response. The completion of the circuit is indicated by the illumination of a light bulb in a miniature socket.

The questions and responses are written on 1″ x 3″ pieces of index cards that are held in place by thumbtacks. Located at each question and response are ⅛″ nuts and bolts. Located at the back of the board is a bell wire connection that joins the question to the correct response. To eliminate unnecessary changing of the back of the board wiring, the board can be turned and the questions and responses mounted in different positions. This prevents students from memorizing correct terminals rather than seeking the correct responses.

It is suggested that students be involved in writing the questions and responses. The length of the nuts and bolts is determined by the thickness of the board used as a base.

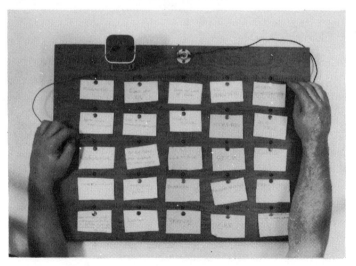

Photo 51

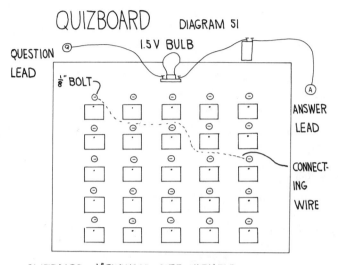

QUIZBOARD DIAGRAM 51

QUIZBOARD - ½" PLYWOOD, SIZE VARIABLE.
CONNECT (Q) TO (A): QUESTION TO CORRECT ANSWER AT BACK
OF BOARD, USE BELL WIRE. A CORRECT ANSWER SHOULD
COMPLETE CIRCUIT AND LIGHT BULB.
IF BULB IS NOT FASTENED, BOARD COULD BE ROTATED
TO FOUR POSITIONS. (MOUNT BULB IN CENTER OF BOARD).
USE 1"× ⅛" NUTS & BOLTS FOR CONNECTING WIRES.
USE THUMB TACKS TO FASTEN Q & A.

CIRCUITS

An electrical circuit is a complete path, consisting of conductors over which an electric current can flow from the source
of electrical energy and back again. Circuits fall into the following classifications:

Series—a method of connecting electrical equipment so that
the current will flow through each device in turn.

Parallel—two circuits connected in such a manner that the
current divides between them.

Series-Parallel—a combination of both series and parallel.

The models illustrate simple circuit boards. The miniature sockets are mounted on a board and the circuit boards are equipped with bulbs and batteries. Insulated copper wire, bared at the ends, connects the miniature sockets and the batteries.

Although two basic circuits are illustrated, many combinations can be constructed by varying the connections and by connecting bells or small motors in the circuits. Care must be taken that the value of the light bulbs compares to the electrical source.

Observations should detect that in a series circuit only one path is available, and a break anywhere in the circuit (removing a bulb) stops the flow of current. In a parallel circuit the current divides, and removing a bulb does not affect the others. In the home, parallel connections enable us to operate each electrical device independently.

Photo 52

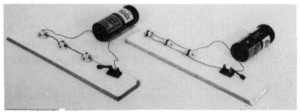

CIRCUITS   DIAGRAM 52

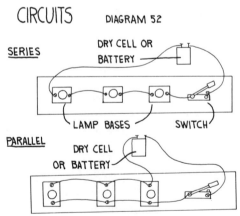

MOUNT LAMP BASES ON WOOD BASE.
USE SINGLE THROW KNIFE SWITCH.
USE CORRECT BULBS TO MATCH VOLTAGE SOURCE.

MECHANICAL GENERATOR

A generator is a device that changes mechanical energy into electrical energy. Generators are based upon the principle that an electromotive force is induced in a conductor when it cuts across magnetic lines of force. This can be accomplished by rotating a coil of wire in a magnetic field (between two magnets), or by rotating the magnet around a stationary coil of wire.

In the model, a horseshoe magnet is mounted vertically by bolting it between two short blocks of wood. The magnet is then placed on a turntable. A coil of wire is wrapped around a wood strip and suspended in the center of the magnet. The coil, which consists of 50 turns of #20 enameled wire, is connected to a galvanometer. The deflection of the needle is noted as the magnet moves around the coil of wire. The motion of the needle changes direction as different poles of the magnet revolve around the coil. This type of generator produces alternating current.

Individual experimentation can focus on changing the construction of the coils (number of turns and diameter of wire), and by changing the speeds of the turntable. The frequency of this alternating current is the same as the number of revolutions made per second by the rotating magnet.

Photo 53

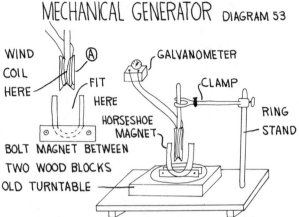

MECHANICAL GENERATOR DIAGRAM 53

WIND COIL HERE — FIT HERE

Ⓐ — GALVANOMETER

CLAMP

BOLT MAGNET BETWEEN
TWO WOOD BLOCKS

HORSESHOE MAGNET

RING STAND

OLD TURNTABLE

COIL - 50 TURNS #20 ENAMELED WIRE ON Ⓐ AND
CONNECT TO GALVANOMETER.
OBSERVE DEFLECTION OF NEEDLE.
VARY SPEEDS OF TURNTABLE.
EXPERIMENT WITH DIFFERENT COILS.
CONNECT LOW POWER BULB TO TERMINALS. (ARGON
   GLOW LAMP).

RESISTANCE BOARD

The possibility of checking math computations with actual measurements in electrical circuits is provided by the resistance board. By using fahnstock clips, any combination of resistance and circuits can be quickly assembled.

This resistance board uses common carbon resistors. Carbon resistors are identified by color bands that indicate the resistance value. There are usually four bands. The first two from one end indicate the first two digits in the resistance value. The third band indicates the number of zeros that follow the first two digits.

Sometimes a fourth band is present. This band indicates tolerance from true value and will be either gold or silver. A gold band indicates a tolerance of 5% and a silver band 10%. If no fourth band is present, the tolerance is 20%.

<u>Colors and Numbers</u>—Each of the colors represents one of the ten digits.

Black	— 0	Orange	— 3	Violet	— 7
Brown	— 1	Yellow	— 4	Gray	— 8
Red	— 2	Green	— 5	White	— 9
		Blue	— 6		

Photo 54

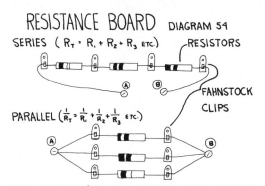

RESISTANCE BOARD DIAGRAM 54

SERIES ($R_T = R_1 + R_2 + R_3$ ETC.) RESISTORS

FAHNSTOCK CLIPS

PARALLEL ($\frac{1}{R_T} = \frac{1}{R_1} + \frac{1}{R_2} + \frac{1}{R_3}$ ETC.)

SERIES-PARALLEL (REDUCE ALL PARALLEL COMPONENTS TO A SINGLE RESISTANCE, THEN USE SERIES FORMULA)

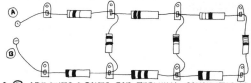

Ⓐ & Ⓑ ARE NUTS & BOLTS FOR TERMINAL CONNECTIONS.
MEASURE ALL RESISTANCES AT Ⓐ & Ⓑ TERMINALS.
FAHNSTOCK CLIPS PERMIT CHANGING RESISTANCES.
MOUNT ON $\frac{1}{4}$" PLYWOOD.

DOOR CHIMES

The objective of this model is to illustrate a type of door chimes installed in many homes. These chimes consist of two horizontally mounted sucking coils (refer to magnetic pile driver). When the push button is depressed, plungers come in contact with metal plates, mounted on rubber gaskets, to produce the sound. Springs return the plungers to the starting position.

Photo 55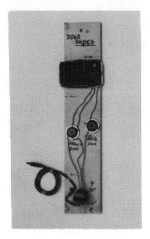

The model is constructed to use line voltage (110 AC) through a step-down transformer to reduce the voltage to 10 volts. Two push buttons are mounted to simulate front and back door locations. One line serves as a return path for both circuits. In residential installations, the transformer is generally mounted on or near a junction box. The primary leads are connected to the line voltage in the junction box while the secondary wires are connected to the chimes.

Care must be taken to completely insulate all the connections with connectors or insulating tape.

DOOR CHIMES   DIAGRAM 55

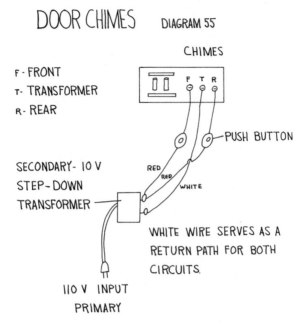

CHIMES

F - FRONT
T- TRANSFORMER
R- REAR

F   T   R

PUSH BUTTON

SECONDARY- 10 V
STEP-DOWN
TRANSFORMER

RED
RED
WHITE

WHITE WIRE SERVES AS A
RETURN PATH FOR BOTH
CIRCUITS.

110 V INPUT
PRIMARY

chapter 6

Demonstrations
with Heat

One of the most indispensable servants of man is heat. We use it to cook our food, extract metals, kill bacteria, and to perform an unlimited number of everyday tasks. Our chief source of heat is the sun, but heat can be obtained in a number of ways (friction, electricity, chemical action, etc.).

The changes of state from a liquid to a gas, from a solid to a liquid, and from a solid to a gas are all dependent upon heat. Man has learned how to generate, control, and put heat to work to improve his standard of living.

Temperature is a measure of the average amount of kinetic energy possessed by each individual molecule of a body and is measured by a thermometer. Many organisms, such as man, maintain a constant body temperature regardless of the changing conditions in his environment. Any deviation from this normal body temperature generally results in a symptom of a physical ailment.

The devices on the following pages provide demonstrations that attempt to illustrate some basic concepts of heat. The substitutions and additions are unlimited insofar as design and demonstration are concerned.

EXPLOSION CAN

The demonstration using the explosion can resembles the gasoline engine in that a fuel is burned in a closed container, resulting in an explosion that forces the lid off the can. The can represents one cylinder of a gasoline engine.

The apparatus requires a one gallon can that has a press-on lid. A hole is punched near the bottom and to the side, large enough that a 3-inch diameter plastic funnel could be pushed through from inside the can. The 6-foot rubber hose is forced on the stem of the funnel that now extends beyond the side of the can.

To demonstrate the explosion, insert a candle in the can opposite the funnel and near the side of the wall of the can. Place some loose cotton in the funnel and place about ½ teaspoon of lycopodium powder on the cotton. Light the candle, press the cover on firmly, and blow into the rubber hose. The powder is forced out of the funnel in a fine spray, combines with the oxygen and is ignited by the candle. The rapid combustion causes the heated air to expand and the lid is forced off the can. If lycopodium powder is not available, powdered corn starch could be heated in a frying pan to dry it out thoroughly and placed in a sealed jar, to use when needed.

The demonstration of rapid combustion can be varied by repeating the demonstration without replacing the lid on the can. The burning fuel results in a large flash. In addition, some powder can be placed in a plastic hose about 2 feet in length and about ½" inside diameter. The powder is then blown across the top of a propane tank or bunsen burner flame and a large flash results. In comparing the explosion can to the gasoline engine, students should note that the power of the explosion can is not controlled, whereas in the gasoline engine the power is converted to mechanical energy.

Photo 56

EXPLOSION CAN   DIAGRAM 56

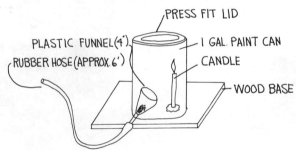

PRESS FIT LID

PLASTIC FUNNEL(4")
RUBBER HOSE (APPROX. 6')

1 GAL. PAINT CAN
CANDLE
WOOD BASE

SET CAN ON WOOD BASE.
PUNCH HOLE ON SIDE, NEAR BOTTOM AND FORCE
FUNNEL IN PLACE. STEM OF FUNNEL SHOULD STICK
OUT OF CAN.
MELT CANDLE & SET CANDLE INTO MELTED WAX.
PLACE SMALL WAD OF COTTON IN BASE OF FUNNEL.
PLACE APPROX. $\frac{1}{2}$ TEASPOON OF LYCOPODIUM POWDER
ON COTTON. LIGHT CANDLE. REPLACE LID AND QUICKLY
BLOW INTO HOSE. EXPLOSION BLOWS LID OFF CAN.
(DRY CORNSTARCH WILL WORK.)
PUNCH SMALL HOLE IN CENTER OF LID.

EXPANSION BAR

The spaces between the ends of steel rails of a railroad track, spaces between concrete sections of a sidewalk or highway, and the slack left in wires when they are strung on telephone poles are only a few of the many examples of precautions taken to allow for expansion of solids when heated.

The expansion bar consists of a rectangular-shaped brass bar fastened at one end to cause expansion in the direction of the indicator. The indicator is a tin strip soldered to a steel rod, but a small dowel stick with a paper indicator will work satisfactorily.

In the demonstration, two propane tanks were held over the brass rod to increase the rate of expansion. As the bar expands, it moves over the indicator rod (or dowel stick) causing it to roll, resulting in the movement of the indicator. As the bar cools, it contracts and the indicator returns to the original position.

A variety of metal bars could be used as substitutes for the brass bar.

Photo 57

EXPANSION BAR   DIAGRAM 57

INDICATOR—SOLDER PIECE OF TIN ONTO 5" NARROW ROD.
HEAT SOURCE- USE I OR 2 BURNERS (PROPANE) ON
BRASS BAR.
EXPANSION OF BAR CAUSES INDICATOR TO TURN.
A ROUND CURTAIN HANGER IS A GOOD SUBSTITUTE FOR
BRASS BAR. USE 2 CANDLES WITH CURTAIN ROD FOR
HEAT SOURCE.

APPROX. SIZE OF INDICATOR DEPENDS UPON SIZE AND
PLACEMENT OF PROTRACTOR.

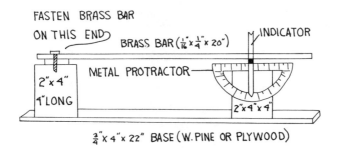

FASTEN BRASS BAR
ON THIS END

BRASS BAR ($\frac{1}{16}$"x$\frac{1}{4}$"x 20")

INDICATOR

METAL PROTRACTOR

2"x 4"
1"LONG

2"x4"x4"

$\frac{3}{4}$"x 4"x 22" BASE (W. PINE OR PLYWOOD)

MOLECULAR MOTION DEMONSTRATOR

There seems to be good reason to believe that all matter is composed of tiny particles known as molecules, and the molecules of all substances are constantly in motion. Molecules of a solid are very close and attract each other, and therefore vibrate in one place. Molecules of a liquid are further apart and can move past each other in all directions within the container, while molecules of a gas move freely in all directions. Evaporation results when a molecule at the surface of a liquid acquires enough kinetic energy to escape from the liquid. The molecular motion device demonstrates all four of the above examples of the behavior of molecules.

The essential parts of the apparatus are transparent materials through which the motion of the spheres (representing molecules) can be viewed. By varying the speed of the motor which regulates the speed of the piston, the spheres can be made to vibrate at speeds which compare to molecular motion in solids, liquids, and gases. When the motor is permitted to run with full voltage (110 AC) the spheres will acquire enough energy to reach the top plastic box. This is intended to represent evaporation.

Many substitutions for spheres are available and probably will work satisfactorily. Good results were obtained by using spherical cork floats or colored ping-pong balls. After considerable experimentation during construction the illustrated device, which measures 26″ in vertical height, resulted in the best combination of parts to provide an excellent working model.

Photo 58

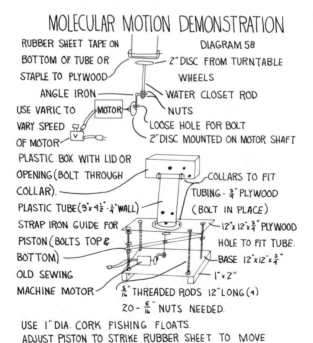

MOLECULAR MOTION DEMONSTRATION

RUBBER SHEET TAPE ON
BOTTOM OF TUBE OR   DIAGRAM 58
STAPLE TO PLYWOOD   2″ DISC FROM TURNTABLE
                           WHEELS
ANGLE IRON   WATER CLOSET ROD
USE VARIC TO MOTOR   NUTS
VARY SPEED   LOOSE HOLE FOR BOLT
OF MOTOR   2″ DISC MOUNTED ON MOTOR SHAFT
PLASTIC BOX WITH LID OR
OPENING (BOLT THROUGH   COLLARS TO FIT
COLLAR).   TUBING - ¾″ PLYWOOD
PLASTIC TUBE (9″x 4½″-¼″ WALL)   (BOLT IN PLACE)
STRAP IRON GUIDE FOR   12″x 12″x ¾″ PLYWOOD
PISTON (BOLTS TOP &   HOLE TO FIT TUBE.
BOTTOM)   BASE 12″x 12″x ¾″
OLD SEWING   1″x 2″
MACHINE MOTOR $\frac{5}{16}$″ THREADED RODS 12″ LONG (4)
            20 - $\frac{6}{16}$″ NUTS NEEDED.
USE 1″ DIA. CORK FISHING FLOATS.
ADJUST PISTON TO STRIKE RUBBER SHEET TO MOVE
CORK SPHERES (•).

THERMOSTAT DEMONSTRATION

The kinetic theory of heat helps us to understand that the collisions of molecules force the molecules to spread farther and farther apart, resulting in the expansion of that substance. All substances—solids, liquids, and gases—generally expand when heated.

Some solids expand faster than others when they are heated. This is illustrated by a compound bar that consists of two unlike strips of metal welded or riveted together. The compound bar is generally made of a strip of iron and a strip of brass fastened together. When the bar is heated the brass side of the bar expands more than the iron, causing the bar to expand unevenly. As the bar cools, it will return to its original position. The bending back and forth of a compound bar finds many applications as a switch in an electrical circuit.

The thermostat is a compound bar designed to control the temperature of a room or a house. The heat present in the room may cause the thermostat to turn on the furnace if the room is too cool, or turn the furnace off if the temperature of the room becomes too warm.

In the demonstration model, the line voltage is connected through a step-down transformer to provide adequate voltage to illuminate two salvaged 12 V automobile taillight bulbs. The compound bar is mounted horizontally but must touch one contact so that one light is always illuminated.

Photo 59

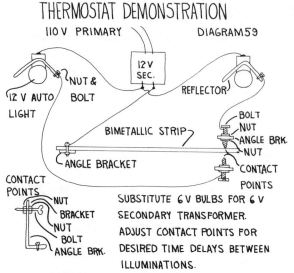

THERMOSTAT DEMONSTRATION

110 V PRIMARY   DIAGRAM 59

12 V SEC.

NUT & BOLT

12 V AUTO LIGHT

REFLECTOR

BIMETALLIC STRIP

BOLT
NUT
ANGLE BRK.
NUT

ANGLE BRACKET

CONTACT POINTS

CONTACT POINTS

NUT
BRACKET
NUT
BOLT
ANGLE BRK.

SUBSTITUTE 6 V BULBS FOR 6 V
SECONDARY TRANSFORMER.
ADJUST CONTACT POINTS FOR
DESIRED TIME DELAYS BETWEEN
ILLUMINATIONS.

HEAT BIMETALLIC STRIP WITH MATCH NEAR END AWAY
FROM CONTACT POINTS. PAINT REFLECTORS DIFFERENT
COLORS. BEND BOTTOM OF REFLECTORS & FASTEN
TO $\frac{3}{4}$" PLYWOOD 8"X 15" APPROX.

CONDUCTOR BAR

In order to make the best possible use of heat, we must learn how to control the heat as it is transferred from one place to another. The transfer of heat is accomplished by conduction in solids, convection in fluids, and radiation by means of heat waves. In a solid, conduction is the transfer of heat by means of the collisions of molecules.

When the end of the conductor bar is placed in a source of heat, the heated molecules at the end of the bar begin to move rapidly. Because of increased motion the molecules collide with their neighbors, causing them to move faster. This process continues until all the molecules of a substance are heated or until an equilibrium is reached where cooling equals heating.

To illustrate conduction, thumbtacks are placed in melted wax on the flat side of the conductor bar at intervals of 2 cm.

One end of the bar is placed in a propane tank flame and the time required for the tacks, located at different distances from the heated end, to fall off is recorded. A graph can be constructed that would plot the time needed to cause the wax to melt to result in the tacks falling off against the distances the tacks are located from the heated end. A variety of metals could be used as a comparative study.

Photo 60

CONDUCTOR BAR DIAGRAM 60

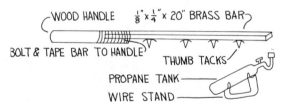

WOOD HANDLE $\frac{1}{8}$"x$\frac{1}{4}$"x 20" BRASS BAR

BOLT & TAPE BAR TO HANDLE

THUMB TACKS

PROPANE TANK

WIRE STAND

MELT CANDLE WAX & PLACE TACKS INTO WAX AT 2" INTERVALS. LET WAX COOL.

PLACE CONDUCTOR IN BURET CLAMP & FASTEN ON RING STAND.

PLACE HEAT SOURCE NEAR END OF BAR & LIGHT TANK.

DRAW GRAPH COMPARING TIME & DISTANCE HEAT TRAVELS UP BAR TO MELT WAX AND CAUSE TACKS TO DROP OFF.

IF AVAILABLE, VARIOUS CONDUCTOR BARS CAN BE MADE FROM DIFFERENT METALS.

BELL THERMOSTAT

The bell thermostat is very similar to the thermostat demonstration and operates under the same principle, but offers an opportunity to work with a 1½ volt battery and a bell. The small compound bar must be mounted in order to complete the circuit when heated by a match.

The contact point consists of a brass bolt filed to a point and held in place by two nuts. Experimentation will indicate best gap distance between the bolt and the compound bar. The contact points can easily be kept clean by holding the compound bar against the contact point and rubbing a book-match cover between the contact point and the compound bar.

In place of the bell, a light bulb can be illuminated when the circuit is completed.

Photo 61

BELL THERMOSTAT DIAGRAM 61

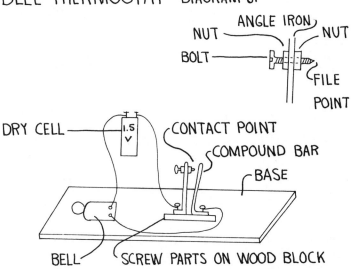

HEAT COMPOUND BAR WITH MATCH TO TOUCH CONTACT POINT AND RING BELL.

CONTACT POINT MUST BE FILED TO A SHARP POINT.

ADJUST GAP FOR BEST RESULTS.

(THERMOSTAT ASSEMBLY MAY BE PURCHASED FROM SCIENCE CATALOGUE).

chapter 7

Ideas for Your
Light Unit

Generally speaking, light is a form of radiant energy received from the sun or other sources, which can act on the eye to induce a visual sensation. Light exhibits two characteristics: (1) It acts as small particles of energy and (2) it exhibits characteristics of waves.

The white light which we receive from the sun is a mixture of all the colors, as was demonstrated by Newton in his experiments using a prism. Light can be separated into its separate components and recombined into white light. This phenomenon is explained by the fact that each wavelength of light actually represents a different color.

Light can be refracted (bent) and reflected (turned back) by substances that have found many applications in optical instruments. Its behavior as it passes through a lens or is reflected in the mirror has led to many scientific discoveries. There is also a very close functional relationship between the eye and the camera.

On the following pages are described a number of projects which can help you to understand the behavior of light. Although there are unlimited demonstrations with optical materials, they all relate to the behavior of light. Experimentation is only a matter of personal interest.

LIGHT BOX

When a light ray passes at an angle from one medium to another (air to glass) it bends and changes direction. This is known as refraction. When light rays strike a surface and are turned back, we say the light rays are reflected. Most of the objects we see are visible because of the light they reflect.

A good demonstration of reflection and refraction can be performed with a light box. The device consists of a rectangular wood box with a glass pane fitted into the top and front sides. The inside is sprayed flat black to provide a good background and reduce reflections. The back side should be left open except for flexible black cloth suspended so that it will cover the entire opening.

In the center of one end, three $\frac{3}{16}''$ holes are drilled approximately one inch apart. A projector is used to project a light beam through the holes into the box. Using touch paper or smoke, the light beams become visible. By placing $4''$ convex and concave lenses in the visible light beam, the refraction of light can be easily seen. A mirror placed in the light beam demonstrates reflection. By moving the angle of the mirror in the light beam, the angle of reflection can be demonstrated. It is also possible to place the convex lens in the light beams and at a further distance place a concave lens in the same light beams, to illustrate converging and diverging light beams.

Photo 62

LIGHT BOX   DIAGRAM 62

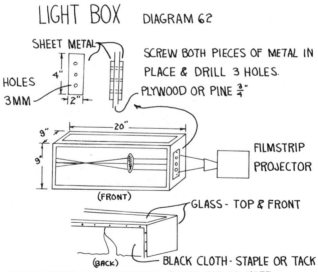

SHEET METAL
HOLES
3MM
4"
2"

SCREW BOTH PIECES OF METAL IN
PLACE & DRILL 3 HOLES.
PLYWOOD OR PINE ¾"

9"
20"
9"
(FRONT)

FILMSTRIP
PROJECTOR

GLASS - TOP & FRONT

(BACK)   BLACK CLOTH - STAPLE OR TACK

TOUCH PAPER OR CIGARETTE SMOKE CAN BE USED.
USE MIRROR & LENS IN LIGHT BOX.
BOX CONSTRUCTION - ¼" PLYWOOD, ¾" PINE ENDS.
GLASS CAN BE TAPED TO EDGES OR FASTENED INSIDE
BOX WITH SMALL ANGLE IRON.
ADJUST POSITION OF PROJECTOR FOR BEST RESULTS.

POLARIZATION OF LIGHT

The wave theory of light is explained by a process called polarization. According to the wave theory, light consists of waves that spread out from a source of light, as do water waves that are formed when a rock is dropped into a pool of water. When a light beam is passed through certain substances, the substances act like parallel slots and will only transmit light vibrations that are parallel to the slots. This polarized light consists of vibrations in only one direction.

The model illustrated attempts to show a transverse wave vibrating in one plane. By placing two grids in opposite directions, the cancellation of light waves can be demonstrated. Many substitutions of materials and sizes are possible. Grids and wave sections cut from ¼ -inch plywood work satisfactorily. The widths of the grids and wave sections should be about 1 inch, in order to be held securely with a clamp and fastened to a ring stand.

Photo 63

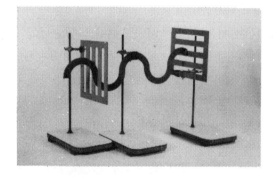

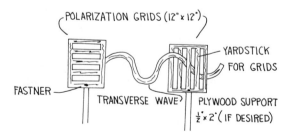

POLARIZATION OF LIGHT DIAGRAM 63

POLARIZATION GRIDS (12" x 12")

YARDSTICK
FOR GRIDS

FASTNER

TRANSVERSE WAVE?

PLYWOOD SUPPORT
½" x 2" (IF DESIRED)

POLARIZATION GRIDS CAN BE MADE FROM SCRAP ALUM.,
CARDBOARD OR YARDSTICKS.
TRANSVERSE WAVE SHOULD BE MADE FROM ALUM.
GRIDS CAN BE CLAMPED ON RING STANDS.
GRIDS CAN BE PLACED PARALLEL BY FASTENING
AT SAME ANGLES TO SUPPORTS.

ROTATING POLARIZER

Polaroid sunglasses use the principle of polarization to cut glare and reflection. Take two pairs of polaroid sunglasses, hold them up in front of you and slowly turn one pair as you look through them. When the glasses are turned so that their crystals are not parallel, they cut out almost all the light.

The rotating polarizer consists of a polarized film mounted in a stationary frame and another film section mounted on the shaft of a slow speed motor. As the motor turns, the light is visible for a few seconds and then the light is blocked from coming through both polaroid sheets.

Many applications of polarization of light can be found in bus windows, camera filters, and sunglasses, in addition to explaining the wave theory of light.

Photo 64

ROTATING POLARIZER DIAGRAM 64

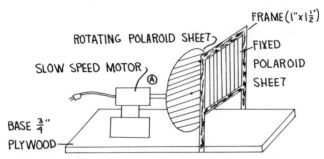

FRAME (1"x1½")

ROTATING POLAROID SHEET

FIXED
POLAROID
SHEET

SLOW SPEED MOTOR

Ⓐ

BASE ¾"
PLYWOOD

SIZE OF FRAME DEPENDS UPON AVAILABLE SIZES
OF POLAROID SHEETS.
SUSPEND A LIGHT (FLASH LIGHT) NEAR MOTOR Ⓐ
& OBSERVE THROUGH FIXED POLAROID SHEET.
ADJUST FIXED POLAROID SHEET SO THAT LIGHT
IS CANCELED OUT WHEN VIEWING AT TOP OF
ROTATION.

PHOTOELECTRIC CELL

When light falls on a surface coated with light-sensitive metal such as cesium, light ejects electrons from these surfaces and they are attracted toward a positive electrode. Light entering the cell generates a current which can find many applications.

One of the most common uses of the photoelectric cell is applied to automatically turning street lights on and off. During the early morning hours the sunlight falls on the photocell, which generates a current and energizes an electromagnet. The electromagnet attracts a piece of metal that acts as a switch and opens the electrical circuit, turning the street light off. The reverse occurs at dusk.

The model illustrated is mounted in a small box with a light bulb inserted in the circuit to represent the street light. By covering the photocell with your hand and removing it, the light bulb is automatically turned off and on. The box serves as storage for the cell and bulbs when not in use.

The photocell used in the demonstration is the type used by the Public Service Electric Company to turn the street lights on and off. They are usually mounted on top of the light.

Photo 65

PHOTOCELL DEMONSTRATION DIAGRAM 65

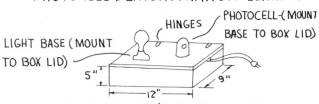

HINGES

PHOTOCELL-(MOUNT BASE TO BOX LID)

LIGHT BASE (MOUNT TO BOX LID)

5"

9"

12"

BOX MADE WITH ½" STOCK, GLUE & TACK

WIRING DIAGRAM

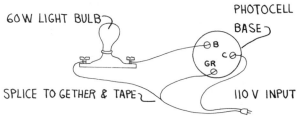

60W LIGHT BULB

PHOTOCELL BASE

B
C
GR

SPLICE TOGETHER & TAPE

110 V INPUT

COVER PHOTOCELL WITH HAND & LIGHT BULB GOES ON.
ALL WIRING DONE INSIDE THE BOX LID.
BOX SERVES AS STORAGE FOR CELL & BULBS.

COPY BOX

The copy box has proved to be a useful aid in correcting diagrams, graphs, maps, and for copying materials. This is easily done by placing the corrected copy on the glass face and then placing the copy to be corrected on top of the correct copy. Any incorrect lines can easily be seen by the light shining through both papers. Some difficulty is experienced using colored papers.

The size of the light box is determined by the size of the glass top. An old television glass is easily adapted because of its size, and most television glass is safety glass. It is not recommended to use window glass. Lucite and plexiglass are good substitutes, but they become scratched with continuous use.

Excellent results were obtained by mounting two 15 W fluorescent lights in the box. (Fluorescent lights produce less heat than incandescent bulbs.) The box was constructed to fit the glass top. A wide substitution of materials is possible for constructing the box.

Again, it should be assumed that someone will accidentally lean on the glass and therefore window glass *is not* recommended.

Photo 66

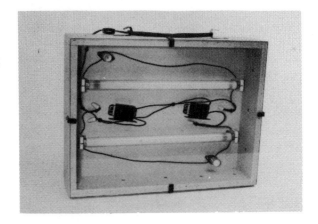

COPY BOX DIAGRAM 66

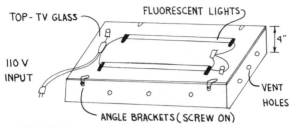

TOP- TV GLASS

FLUORESCENT LIGHTS

110 V INPUT

4"

VENT HOLES

ANGLE BRACKETS (SCREW ON)

PROCEDURE

OBTAIN DESIRED SIZE OLD TV GLASS.
OBTAIN FLUORESCENT LIGHTS (ONE MAY BE ENOUGH).
CONSTRUCT BOX ($\frac{3}{4}$" STOCK) SIZE TO FIT GLASS EVENLY.
INSTALL LIGHTS, BALLAST, STARTERS, ETC.
SPRAY INSIDE OF BOX LIGHT COLOR.
FASTEN GLASS TO BOX WITH SMALL ANGLE BRACKETS.
(GLASS CAN BE REMOVED TO SERVICE LIGHTS.)
USES - CORRECTING MAPS, DIAGRAMS, COPYING
MATERIALS, ETC.

PINHOLE CAMERA

In order to see an object, light must travel from the object to the eye. This illustrates the fact that light travels in a straight line and explains why we cannot see around corners and why objects cast shadows.

The pinhole camera consists of an oatmeal container having a pinhole in the middle of the bottom. The inside of the container is sprayed black. When a candle is placed a short distance from the pinhole, the light will enter the pinhole and form an image on the wax paper. Since light travels in straight lines, a ray of light that starts out from the top of the candle flame will strike the lower part of the wax paper. The ray from the bottom of the candle flame will strike the wax paper at the upper part, resulting in an inverted image of the candle flame on the wax paper. The pinhole camera should be moved closer or away from the flame to obtain a clear image.

The screen for viewing the image is easily constructed by cutting a hole in the top section of the box, placing wax paper over the open end, and replacing the top on the container to hold the wax paper in place.

Photo 67

PINHOLE CAMERA DIAGRAM 67

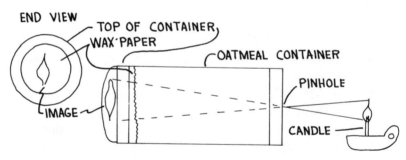

CUT HOLE (3" DIA.) IN TOP OF CONTAINER.
PLACE WAX PAPER OVER TOP OF CONTAINER.
PLACE TOP OF OATMEAL CONTAINER OVER WAX PAPER.
TAPE TOP TO HOLD WAX PAPER SCREEN IN PLACE.
SPRAY-PAINT INSIDE OF CONTAINER BLACK.
MOVE CONTAINER TOWARDS OR AWAY FROM FLAME
TO OBTAIN IMAGE ON WAX PAPER SCREEN.

COLOR BY ADDITION

All the colors that we see are produced by mixing red, blue, and green in the right proportions. These are called the primary colors. It is believed that the eye is equipped with three sets of nerves—each of which is sensitive to one of the primary colors.

A transparent body, such as a piece of colored plastic, selectively transmits its own color and absorbs the other colors. If white light is passed through a green piece of plastic, only the green portion of the spectrum will be transmitted.

In the demonstrations illustrated, three pieces of plexiglass (red, blue, and green) were placed in front of three projectors of equal wattage (same size projection bulb) and the colors projected on a screen. By moving the projectors to make the colors overlap, the following combinations can be obtained:

Red and Green	=	Yellow
Blue and Red	=	Magenta
Blue and Green	=	Blue-green
All Colors	=	White

Photo 68

After considerable experimentation, excellent results were obtained with pieces of red, blue, and green pieces of plexiglass obtained from—

McKilligan
Industrial Supply
Maine, New York 13802

COLOR BY ADDITION   DIAGRAM 68

RED + GREEN ⟶ YELLOW
BLUE+ RED ⟶ MAGENTA
BLUE+ GREEN ⟶ BLUE-GREEN
ALL COLORS ⟶ WHITE

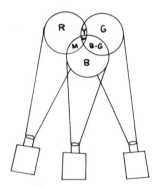

USE 3 FILMSTRIP PROJECTORS WITH THE SAME WATTAGE.
FOR BEST RESULTS USE PLEXIGLASS (RED, GREEN, BLUE)
McKILLIGAN
INDUSTRIAL SUPPLY CORP.
MAINE, N.Y. 13802

chapter 8

Improve Your Teaching
of Life Science

The opportunities for investigations in Life Science are unlimited. The focus of this chapter is on ideas and materials that can be reused constantly.

The greenhouse offers an opportunity for germinating seeds all year round. The sugar and ATP molecules will probably remain with us indefinitely unless major biological discoveries prove present theories to be incorrect. The DNA molecule model clearly illustrates its structure, and its construction provides durability as well as easy storage.

The hydroponics experiment can be attempted by many students because construction is not limited to the illustrated sizes. The mitosis and meiosis display boards help students to understand cell reproduction through a visual illustration of a difficult concept. The smoking demonstration enables students to actually sample the unhealthful products of cigarette smoke.

Because of the problems faced by teachers in stimulating pupil interest, it is hoped that the life science teaching ideas in this chapter will provide students with interesting ideas and motivation for further investigations.

GREENHOUSE

Although substitution of materials is encouraged, the overall construction of the greenhouse is governed by the size of available trays. A variety of inexpensive plastic trays are available that vary in length and width. It is suggested that a tray have a minimum depth of two inches for germinating plants.

Reasonably good success is obtained with a mixture that consists of ⅓ peat moss, ⅓ sand, and ⅓ humus. The procedure used was to make a furrow approximately ¼-inch deep in the soil with a pencil, place the seeds in the furrow, and cover the seeds with a fine layer of sand. The plants find less resistance breaking through the sand than the soil.

Photo 69

When the germinating plants break the soil, the door must be removed or kept open. The purpose is to prevent excessive stem growth and encourage root growth. When the second set of leaves appear, it is time for transplanting each individual plant into containers that provide sufficient room for growth.

GREENHOUSE DIAGRAM 69

BOTTOM, SIDES & TOP SECTIONS MADE FROM 4" X $\frac{3}{4}$" STOCK.
FRONT COVER 1" X 2" FRAME. CORNER SUPPORTS $\frac{1}{4}$" PLYWOOD.
USE HEAVY CLEAR PLASTIC. STAPLE PLASTIC TO FRAME
AND TACK $\frac{1}{8}$" X 1" STRIP ON PLASTIC, COVER ALL SIDES.
USE FLUORESCENT LIGHT TO REDUCE HEAT.
HINGE DOOR (FRONT COVER) TO OPEN FROM BOTTOM.
SIZE MAY BE VARIED.

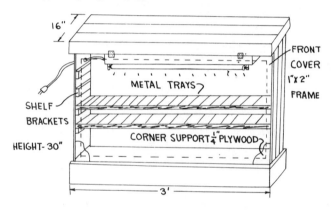

ATP MOLECULE

Adenosine triphosphate is a molecule that supplies the energy required for cellular activities. All cells obtain their energy from the phosphate bonds of the ATP molecule and all cells manufacture their own ATP.

The ATP molecule consists of an adenosine molecule and three phosphate groups. These phosphate groups appear to form a three-unit section bonded to the adenosine molecule. The breaking of the bond between the second and the third phosphate groups releases a considerable amount of energy, which is utilized by the cell in various ways.

The objective of the model is an attempt to present a visual picture of its bonding structure and the location and composition of the phosphate groups. The model is made with 1-inch diameter spheres and the different atoms are color coded by painting with water base paint before mounting on a display board.

Photo 70

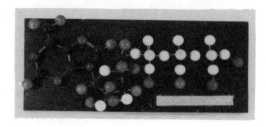

ATP MOLECULE   DIAGRAM 70

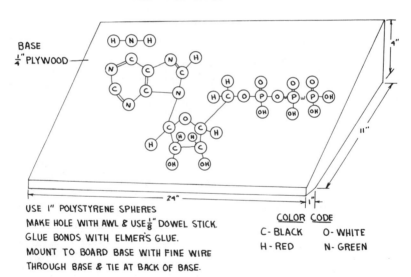

USE I" POLYSTYRENE SPHERES
MAKE HOLE WITH AWL & USE ⅛" DOWEL STICK.
GLUE BONDS WITH ELMER'S GLUE.
MOUNT TO BOARD BASE WITH FINE WIRE
THROUGH BASE & TIE AT BACK OF BASE.

COLOR CODE
C - BLACK   O - WHITE
H - RED   N - GREEN

SUGAR MOLECULES

Carbohydrates are composed of molecules called simple sugars. Two of the most important sugars are glucose and fructose. Both of these molecules have the same chemical formula ($C_6H_{12}O_6$), yet they are different. Looking closely at the diagram and the models you will notice that the structural arrangement of each molecule is different, which gives the molecule different characteristics. It should be evident that glucose is composed of a six atom ring while fructose is composed of a five atom ring.

Both models were mounted in a nearly vertical position so that the ring structures are easily compared. The size and construction of the molecules is dependent upon the size of spheres available, but identical sizes should be used for identical atoms. The atoms are held together with ⅛" dowel sticks dipped into white glue and inserted into holes punched in the spheres with a nail.

Sucrose, common table sugar, is a carbohydrate made of the two simple sugar units, glucose and fructose.

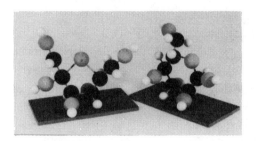

Photo 71

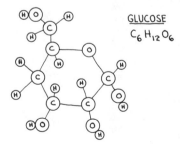

SUGAR MOLECULES DIAGRAM 71

GLUCOSE
$C_6H_{12}O_6$

FRUCTOSE
$C_6H_{12}O_6$

DIAMETERS

2" - Ⓒ - CARBON (BLACK)   USE ⅛" DOWEL STICKS FOR
2" - Ⓞ - OXYGEN (RED)   BONDS. PUNCH HOLE WITH
1" - Ⓗ - HYDROGEN (WHITE)   NAIL & GLUE WITH
                            ELMER'S GLUE.

MEIOSIS AND MITOSIS

The meiosis and mitosis display boards were constructed with "pop" plastic beads mounted on 18" x 36" ceiling tiles. The phases of mitosis use a variety of small colored beads that were strung on fine wire, fastened through the tile and tied at the back. The grouping of the beads was intended to represent chromosomes. The beads were intended to represent genes.

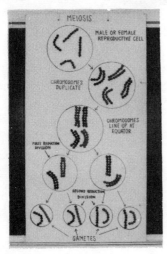
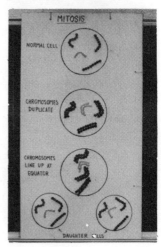

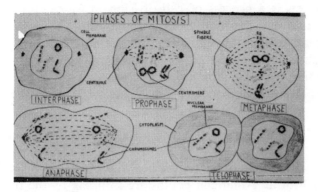

Photo 72

To simplify construction different sets of colored beads were used, which eliminated the need for painting the beads. Different phases of cell division were identified by labeling with a permanent marker.

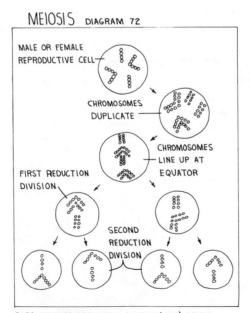

MEIOSIS DIAGRAM 72

MALE OR FEMALE
REPRODUCTIVE CELL

CHROMOSOMES
DUPLICATE

CHROMOSOMES
LINE UP AT
EQUATOR

FIRST REDUCTION
DIVISION

SECOND
REDUCTION
DIVISION

CHROMOSOMES MADE FROM PLASTIC 'POP' BEADS.
FASTEN WITH FINE WIRE TO COLORED CEILING TILE.

Meiosis is a process of cell division in which the resulting cells contain half the number of chromosomes. The cells which undergo meiosis are the egg and sperm cells.

Mitosis is a process of cell division in which the resulting cells contain the same number of chromosomes as the parent cell. The offspring of a human receives 23 pairs of chromosomes.

SMOKING MACHINE

Smoking is one of the largest health problems in the country. About half of all American youths are smoking by the time they become 18. Almost every child experiments with smoking. While some stop, others continue smoking.

The purpose of this experiment is to point out the effects of smoking. The jar in this experiment is half filled with water. A cigarette is torn apart and placed in the pipe bowl. Using the hand aspirator, the smoke is drawn from the cigarette into the water in the jar. After the cigarette is burned completely, examine the color of the water and taste the liquid.

A ball-point barrel could be substituted for the pipe. The cigarette can be mounted directly in the barrel. A cotton pad could be used to filter the smoke and collect the accumulation of tar. The cotton should be passed around the room for the students to observe and smell.

Photo 73

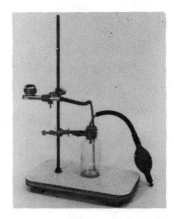

SMOKING MACHINE DIAGRAM 73

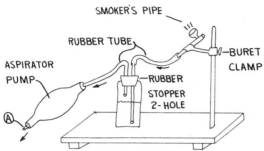

SMOKER'S PIPE

RUBBER TUBE

ASPIRATOR PUMP

—BURET CLAMP

—RUBBER STOPPER 2-HOLE

Ⓐ

USE 8 OZ. WIDE-MOUTH COLLECTING BOTTLE.
USE $\frac{1}{4}$" (O.D.) COPPER OR ALUMINUM TUBE AND CONNECT
WITH RUBBER TUBE.
FILL COLLECTING BOTTLE $\frac{3}{4}$ FULL. OPERATE HAND
ASPIRATOR. LIQUID COLLECTS WASTE PRODUCTS
NORMALLY INHALED BY SMOKER.
CONNECT ASPIRATOR TO PIPE. COLLECT WASTE
PRODUCT ON PAPER TOWEL AT ASPIRATOR EXIT Ⓐ.

DNA MOLECULE

Deoxyribonucleic acid—the master molecule that designs all other molecules. It is an acid that is located in the nucleus of every cell. This molecule directs the process of life in every organism. The main function of the molecule is the transmission of the genetic code from parent to offspring. It also directs the metabolism (day to day activities of the cell).

Although the molecule is composed of thousands of atoms, it contains only 6 submolecular building blocks.

Deoxyribose	alternating units that represent uprights
Phosphate	of the double helix

Adenine ⎫
Thymine ⎭ ⎧ pairs of bases that represent the rungs of
Guanine ⎫ ⎩ the ladder
Cytosine ⎭

The features of the two illustrated models are the effectiveness as teaching aids and the extremely low cost of construction. Both models were constructed from ¾″ scraps of hardwood, a steel rod, small hose, round head pins, and coat-hanger wire.

It is suggested that all pieces used in construction be drilled prior to any assembly. A supporting rod of ⁵⁄₁₆″ is suggested. The length of the rod is determined by the number of base units and overall height of the model desired. The illustration depicts models of approximately 24 inches in height. A steel washer is used as a spacer between each base on the steel rod.

Any combintion of bases is possible, but they must remain the same size throughout the model. The connecting wire that holds the base pairs together represents the hydrogen bonds. Any color combinations are satisfactory substitutes, but they must remain consistent. Additional activities can involve construction of an RNA section fastened to one hose, which can be placed on the model to illustrate the function of the RNA.

Photo 74

Constructed from an idea suggested by Richard E. McKeeby, instructor of biology, Union Jr. College, Cranford, N.J.

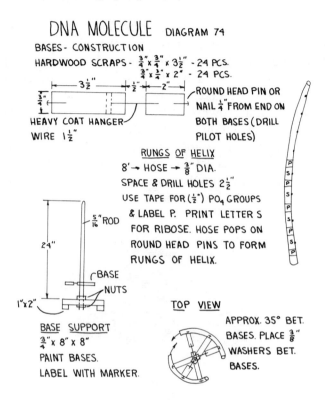

DNA MOLECULE DIAGRAM 74

BASES - CONSTRUCTION

HARDWOOD SCRAPS - $\frac{3}{4}'' \times \frac{3}{4}'' \times 3\frac{1}{2}''$ - 24 PCS.
$\frac{3}{4}'' \times \frac{3}{4}'' \times 2''$ - 24 PCS.

3½" ½" 2" ROUND HEAD PIN OR
$\frac{3}{4}$ NAIL $\frac{1}{4}''$ FROM END ON
HEAVY COAT HANGER BOTH BASES (DRILL
WIRE 1½" PILOT HOLES)

RUNGS OF HELIX

8' → HOSE → $\frac{3}{8}''$ DIA.
SPACE & DRILL HOLES 2½"
USE TAPE FOR (½") PO₄ GROUPS
& LABEL P. PRINT LETTER S
FOR RIBOSE. HOSE POPS ON
ROUND HEAD PINS TO FORM
RUNGS OF HELIX.

$\frac{5}{16}''$ ROD

24"

BASE
NUTS

1"x2"

BASE SUPPORT
$\frac{3}{4}'' \times 8'' \times 8''$
PAINT BASES.
LABEL WITH MARKER.

TOP VIEW

APPROX. 35° BET.
BASES. PLACE $\frac{3}{8}''$
WASHERS BET.
BASES.

HYDROPONICS

The science of hydroponics provides a method for growing plants by water culture or nutrient culture (without soil). All nutrient solutions contain basically potassium, calcium, magnesium, nitrates, phosphates, and sulfates. It is suggested that commercially prepared nutrient solutions be purchased.

Although many types of containers can be used, the illustrated apparatus produced excellent results. The bed was constructed from discarded screen wire. Additional larger holes were made using a nail to provide for root growth into the solution. The bed (wire basket) was placed in an aquarium and suspended with wire hooks. A 1-inch layer of large vermiculite flakes were placed in the bed and the seeds were placed in the vermiculite.

The seeds were watered twice daily with the nutrient solution, which was placed in a sprinkler bottle (type used to dampen clothes while ironing), and a glass plate was placed on the aquarium. When the seeds begin to germinate, place the nutrient solution in the container to a height that nearly touches the wire basket. Care must be taken that the glass plate be removed to prevent mold from growing in the container. It is suggested to stir the nutrient solution daily without disturbing the young plants, and also to change the solution weekly. This can be done by using a siphon. This activity provides an opportunity for students to observe root growth and serves as a supply of root sections for microscope observations.

Photo 75

HYDROPONICS   DIAGRAM 75

CONTAINER - 2 GAL. AQUARIUM

WIRE HOOK
(EACH CORNER)   SCREEN BASKET

SOLUTION

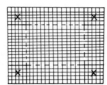

SCRAP SCREEN WIRE
TO FIT INSIDE
CONTAINER

CUT OUT SECTIONS MARKED 'X'.
BEND ALONG DOTTED LINES TO FORM CONTAINER FOR
VERMICULITE.
LACE CORNERS WITH FINE COPPER WIRE.
MAKE 4 HOOKS WITH HEAVY WIRE TO SUPPORT THE
SCREEN BASKET IN HYDROPONICS SOLUTION.
(THIS IDEA CAN BE ADAPTED TO ANY SIZE OR SHAPE
CONTAINER.)

chapter 9

Experiences with Working Machines

Man is constantly at work trying to adapt to his environment to serve his needs. In performing this work, man encounters many situations that require more speed and strength than he can physically furnish. A machine does not save a man any work but it can make his work easier in the following ways:

1. The machine can multiply the force applied to it, making it possible to overcome a large obstacle by applying a small force.
2. The machine can increase the speed with which a given job is done.

In every machine we deal with the forces of "effort" and "resistance." The effort is the force applied by the man to the machine and the resistance is the obstacle he is trying to overcome or the weight he is trying to lift. The ratio of the resistance overcome by a machine to the effort applied is called the "mechanical advantage" of that machine. It is expressed as—

$$\text{Mechanical Advantage} \quad = \quad \frac{\text{Resistance}}{\text{Effort}}$$

Although the machine enables a man to do his work easier, a man pays for this advantage because it is balanced by the additional distance man must move to accomplish a given task. It must also be remembered that no machine is perfect and that some of the work put into the machine is always wasted in overcoming friction.

BALANCE BEAM

The balance beam is essentially a bar that is free to turn on a pivot. The horizontal arm should be graduated in equal divisions from the center. A variety of weights can be used at various distances to make the beam balance. The students can complete mathematically the formula F x D = F x D (F = force and D = distance) and predetermine what weights would be required to balance the beam at what distance.

Lead sinkers with identifying weights were used successfully, although substitutions are adaptable.

Photo 76

BALANCE BEAM DIAGRAM 76

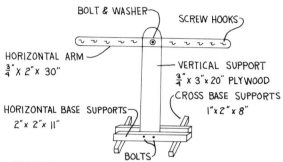

BOLT & WASHER

SCREW HOOKS

HORIZONTAL ARM
$\frac{3}{4}$" X 2" X 30"

VERTICAL SUPPORT
$\frac{3}{4}$" X 3" X 20" PLYWOOD

CROSS BASE SUPPORTS
1" X 2" X 8"

HORIZONTAL BASE SUPPORTS
2" X 2" X 11"

BOLTS

PROCEDURE

BOLT OR NAIL HORIZONTAL BASE SUPPORTS THRU VERTICAL SUPPORT.

PLACE SCREW HOOKS AT EQUAL DISTANCES FROM CENTER.

IMPROVISE BOLT & WASHER ASSEMBLY TO REDUCE FRICTION.

LEAD SINKERS (WITH OZ. MARKINGS) CAN BE USED AS WEIGHTS.

CROSS BASE SUPPORTS PREVENT TIPPING.

MECHANICAL CARTS

Adaptable to many experiments, the mechanical cart is easily and inexpensively constructed. The pegboard top provides holes for quickly fastening various masses. The eye hooks provide a point at which a scale can be fastened for experiments relating to acceleration and the inclined plane.

Photo 77

A variation of the cart can be constructed by substituting various sized bolts for axles in place of the roller skate axle. It is also suggested that the wheel surfaces be relatively smooth to reduce friction.

MECHANICAL CARTS   DIAGRAM 77

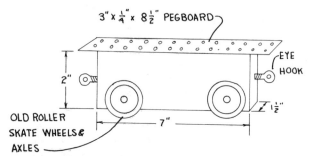

DRILL HOLES 1" FROM END & ½" FROM BOTTOM FOR AXLE
OF ROLLER SKATE.
USE VENETIAN BLIND CHORD FOR TIEING WEIGHTS TO
PEGBOARD AND FOR PULLING CART.
OIL SKATE WHEELS TO REDUCE FRICTION.
CART SIZES MAY BE VARIED BY USING DIFFERENT
SIZE NUTS & BOLTS IN PLACE OF SKATE AXLE.

BALANCE BAR LEVER

The balance bar lever is essentially the same as the balance beam, with a few variations. In place of using hooks, tuna cans are used to hold smaller objects. In addition, the pivot can be moved to change the lengths of the arms. The cans are also adjustable by simply removing the bolt and moving the can to another pre-drilled hole.

Again, the math aspect of the teaching aid should be emphasized in any experiments with the balance bar lever.

Photo 78

BALANCE BAR LEVER   DIAGRAM 78

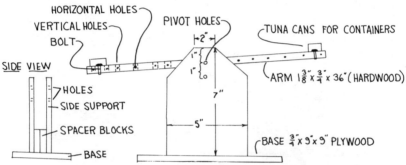

DRILL EVENLY SPACED VERTICAL HOLES FOR DIFFERENT CONTAINER POSITIONS.
DRILL EVENLY SPACED HORIZONTAL HOLES FOR DIFFERENT ARM POSITIONS.
USE LARGE NAIL OR ROD FOR PIVOT.
DRILL HORIZONTAL HOLES CORRECT SIZE TO FIT NAIL OR ROD.
(I USED $\frac{1}{4}$" HOLES & 16 PENNY COMMON NAIL WITH THE POINT GROUND OFF.)
BE SURE ARM BALANCES. LEAD SINKERS WORK WELL AS WEIGHTS.

FRICTION BLOCK

The force that opposes the movement of one body over another is called friction. A body which rolls over another body
encounters less opposition from friction than if it were sliding

over the same surface. Friction is affected by the following factors:

1. The rougher the surfaces, the greater will be the friction.
2. The greater the pressure forcing the two surfaces together, the greater will be the friction.
3. Friction is usually greater when forces are just beginning to slide over each other than when they are already in motion.

It must be remembered that there are advantages as well as disadvantages of friction.

With the friction block, a scale could be used to measure effort necessary to overcome friction of various surfaces. Both the smooth and rough side could be used. In addition, dowel sticks could be placed under the block as well as additional weights placed on the friction block.

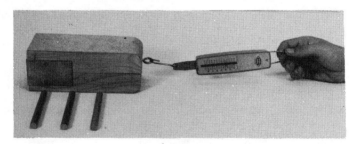

Photo 79

FRICTION BLOCK   DIAGRAM 79

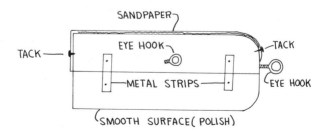

BLOCK MADE FROM 2 PIECES 2"x4" SCRAPS FASTENED
TOGETHER. LENGTH APROX. 8"
FASTEN TOGETHER WITH METAL STRIPS.
EYE HOOKS ON SIDES FOR ATTACHING ADDITIONAL
WEIGHTS.

WHEEL AND AXLE

This machine consists of a large wheel, which is attached to a smaller wheel or axle. Both wheels turn together. By applying effort to the large wheel, a large resistance can be overcome on the small wheel. (Example—the door knob, steering wheels of automobiles, etc.) In some wheel and axle combinations, the effort is applied to the small wheel in order to gain speed (example—wheel of a bicycle).

If difficulty is encountered in fastening the various wheels on the axle, a ⅝" threaded rod could be used and bolts on each side of the wooden wheels will keep them from slipping. Some kind of bearing must be devised to reduce the friction of the axle.

Photo 80

The student can place the weight on any of the wheels and, using a scale, he can measure the effort required to lift any combination of weights. The math formula for this machine is

$$\frac{R}{E} = \frac{\text{Radius of wheel}}{\text{Radius of axle}}.$$

When using the handle to turn the machine, this represents the wheel in the experiments and any of the wheels will represent the axles.

WHEEL AND AXLE   DIAGRAM 80

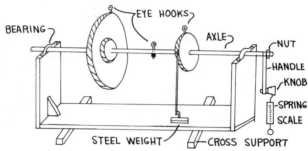

IMPROVISE BEARINGS TO REDUCE FRICTION.
WHEELS ARE WOOD WITH CENTER GROOVE. (CARRIAGE
WHEELS TACK-WELDED TO AXLE WORK WELL).
SIZE OF BASE DETERMINED BY SIZE OF WHEELS AND
AXLE.
FRAME MADE FROM $\frac{3}{4}$" x 5" WHITE PINE OR SUBSTITUTE.
HANDLE FASTENED TO AXLE WITH NUT. (VARIOUS LENGTH
HANDLES COULD BE USED.)

ACCELERATION RAMP

Acceleration is the gain in speed of a body per unit of time. Using the ramp model, students can roll spheres of various masses and compare the acceleration. These are examples of uniform acceleration where the sphere's speed is increased by the same speed every second.

By placing various objects in the path of the accelerating spheres, we can observe the effect of collisions caused by the accelerating spheres. Various masses and shaped objects can be placed as collision objects. In addition, the height of the ramp support can be varied by using books or blocks to vary or compare the experiments.

The "V" groove ramp can be purchased at a lumber yard, where it is sold as wood corner molding.

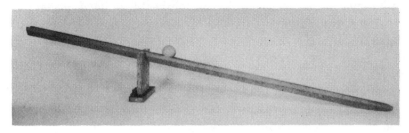

Photo 81

ACCELERATION RAMP DIAGRAM 81

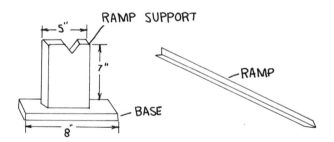

BASE - $\frac{3}{4}''$ x 3" x 8" PLYWOOD.

SUPPORT - $\frac{3}{4}''$ x 5" x 7" PLYWOOD (SIZE MAY VARY).

RAMP - MADE FROM 2 PIECES $\frac{1}{2}''$ x 1" x 3" (2 PIECES
OF WOOD TRIM CAN BE NAILED TOGETHER.)
CUT EXIT END ON ANGLE TO MAKE SMOOTH
FIT WITH TABLE OR FLOOR.

USE VARIOUS SIZE AND TYPE SPHERES (STEEL,
MARBLES, ETC.).

PULLEY RACK

The pulley is a grooved wheel supported in a frame. It can be fastened by means of a hook to a fixed beam (fixed pulley), or it may be fastened to a resistance (movable pulley). Pulleys are used in various combinations to lift heavy objects with relatively small forces.

Since many strands of rope hold up the resistance in a pulley system, each strand must share in supporting the total weight. Since a pulley system multiplies the effort that is applied, it does this at the expense of distance. The mathematical relationship can be expressed as follows—

$$\text{Effort} \quad = \quad \frac{\text{Resistance}}{\text{Number of Strands}}$$

Photo 82

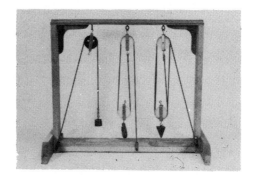

The pulley rack illustrated presents a variety of pulley combinations. A spring scale could be used to verify mathematical computations relating to the effort required to overcome a resistance. A variety of weights could be used as resistances.

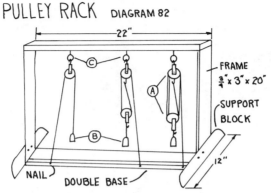

PULLEY RACK DIAGRAM 82

Ⓐ - DOUBLE PULLEYS.
Ⓑ - WEIGHTS (LEAD SINKERS OR SUBSTITUTE).
Ⓒ - EYE HOOKS.
USE SPRING SCALE IN EXPERIMENTS.
SUPPORT BLOCKS PREVENT TIPPING.
PULLEYS ARE 2" PLASTIC (SUBSTITUTIONS O.K.).

RESILIENCY TESTER

This simple device provides an unlimited opportunity for individual experiments. In addition to a variety of spheres that can be dropped down the tube, a variety of substances could be used in place of the metal base. Suggested are experiments with metal, wood, plastic, or stone bases. In addition, a variety of floor covering combinations can be used such as outdoor carpet, indoor carpet, carpet with rubber and/or hair padding, and hard surface floor coverings.

A graph can be constructed to illustrate the resiliency of the various materials on the different bases.

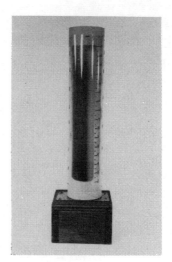

Photo 83

RESILIENCY TESTER DIAGRAM 83

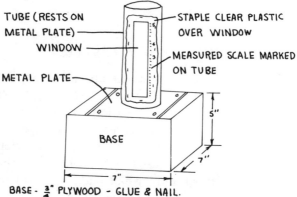

TUBE (RESTS ON METAL PLATE)

STAPLE CLEAR PLASTIC OVER WINDOW

WINDOW

MEASURED SCALE MARKED ON TUBE

METAL PLATE

BASE

5"

7"

7"

BASE - $\frac{3}{4}$" PLYWOOD - GLUE & NAIL.
SCREW METAL PLATE TO TOP OF BASE.
TUBE - LINOLEUM TUBE 4" DIA. x 20".
WINDOW - $2\frac{1}{2}$" x 15" (MEASURE SCALE WITH MARKER.
VARIOUS TYPES OF SPHERES CAN BE DROPPED DOWN
THE TUBE & MEASURED FOR RESILIENCY. SUBSTITUTE
MATERIAL CAN BE PLACED ON METAL PLATE.

ALL-PURPOSE SUPPORT

A simple device that lends itself to a number of demonstrations can be easily and inexpensively constructed. The device lends itself to suspending pulleys, springs, and pendulum experiments. It should be noted that the top bracket is longer than the bottom. This permits the support to be placed on a desk and experimental materials can be suspended beyond the edge of the desk. It may be necessary to clamp the support to the desk with large "C" clamps if heavy materials are suspended during experiments.

Photo 84

ALL-PURPOSE SUPPORT DIAGRAM 84

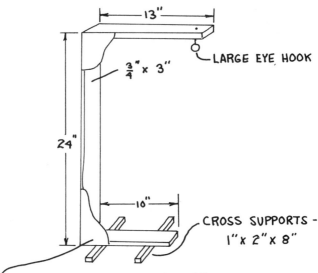

13"

$\frac{3}{4}$" x 3"

LARGE EYE HOOK

24"

10"

CROSS SUPPORTS -
1"x 2"x 8"

REINFORCE CORNERS WITH $\frac{1}{4}$" PLYWOOD

USES - SUSPEND SCALES, PULLEYS OR ANY TYPE
DEMONSTRATION MATERIAL.

chapter 10

Vibrating Devices
You Can Make

Sound is one of the basic factors in our environment because it enables us to communicate ideas through the medium of the spoken word. Among the thousands of sounds that we hear each day, unfortunately many bring nervous strain and annoyance. Many sounds—such as the movement of the wind, songs of the birds, and roll of thunder—are examples of sounds in nature. One of man's artistic forms of expression is music. Bodies that vibrate at a definite frequency produce a musical tone. The opposite is characteristic of noise.

All sounds are produced by vibrating bodies. The number of times a body vibrates is called its frequency. Although most sounds are transmitted through the air to our ears, any substance, whether solid, liquid, or gas, can transmit sound. Sound cannot pass through a vacuum.

Because sound travels about 1100 feet per second, a roar of thunder always comes after a flash of lightning. We can approximate the distance where the lightning occurred by counting the seconds between the flash and the thunder. Five seconds of time approximates one mile in distance.

TRANSFER OF ENERGY

Sound is transmitted through a medium by longitudinal waves, which cause the particles of a medium to vibrate parallel to the direction in which the wave is moving. When sound waves pass through air, they cause the air molecules to vibrate. These vibrating air molecules in turn cause the eardrum to vibrate and make us aware of the sound.

Referring to the model, balls of approximately equal size and mass (clackers) are suspended by light cords in a position where they barely touch each other. If we lift one of the spheres located at either end and release it, a pulse of compression will travel through the spheres, with the result that the last sphere will be displaced from its original position a distance almost as far as the initial sphere was lifted. This effect is the result of a transfer of energy from molecule to molecule, which attempts to illustrate how sound is transferred.

Photo 85

TRANSFER of ENERGY DIAGRAM 85

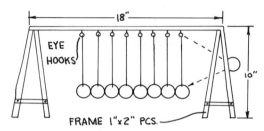

HANG SPHERES SO THAT THEY TOUCH.
SPHERES USED WERE DONATED "CLICK-CLAKS".
LIFT SPHERE AT ONE END & RELEASE.
SPHERE ON OPPOSITE END WILL BE DEFLECTED
BY TRANSFER OF ENERGY.
TRY RELEASING VARIOUS COMBINATIONS.

SONOMETER

Musical instruments utilize vibrating strings which are bowed, struck, or plucked by finger or pick. Music is also produced by vibration of air columns in wind instruments.

If we keep picking a guitar string while shortening its length, the sound becomes higher. The reverse also occurs. The highness or lowness of a sound is known as pitch, which can be affected in the following ways:

1. Length of the string
2. Thickness of the string
3. How tightly the string is fastened

Using the sonometer, all three of the above conditions can be demonstrated. A variety of bridges can be used (round bars, wood blocks, etc.). Strings are generally obtained from students, who broke them using stringed instruments. It is also suggested that some type of "box" be used as a mounting surface to produce a louder sound.

Photo 86

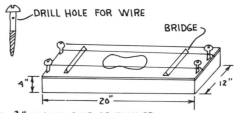

SONOMETER   DIAGRAM 86

DRILL HOLE FOR WIRE

BRIDGE

4"

12"

20"

SIDES- ¾" WHITE PINE OR THICKER.
TOP & BOTTOM - ¼" PLYWOOD.
USE SHEET METAL SCREWS. DRILL SMALL HOLES IN
SCREWS TO FIT & TIGHTEN STRINGS.
MAKE BRIDGES TO FIT UNDER STRINGS FROM
SCRAP ALUMINUM OR SUBSTITUTE.
CUT HOLE IN TOP PIECE OF PLYWOOD.
USE BROKEN STRINGS FROM MUSIC DEPARTMENT
INSTRUMENTS.
SLIDE BRIDGES TO VARY PITCH.

DOPPLER EFFECT

Sound from an approaching source is shorter in wavelength and thus higher in pitch than if it were in a fixed position. (This is experienced by listening to a train's whistle as it approaches or trucks as they pass you by.) As the source recedes, the pitch is lower. This is called the Doppler shift.

Using the model, connect the battery to make the bell ring. Have the students form a large circle outside the classroom and begin swinging the model in larger circles by holding the heavy cord. Students should detect a rise in pitch as the model approaches. The same effect can be obtained using an electric razor, provided that precautions be taken so that the razor will remain attached to some kind of cord.

Photo 87

DOPPLER EFFECT DIAGRAM 87

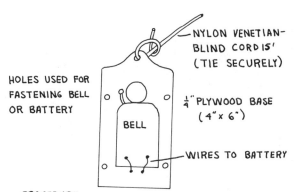

NYLON VENETIAN-
BLIND CORD 15'
(TIE SECURELY)

HOLES USED FOR
FASTENING BELL
OR BATTERY

$\frac{1}{4}$" PLYWOOD BASE
(4"x 6")

BELL

WIRES TO BATTERY

PROCEDURE
TAPE $1\frac{1}{2}$ V BATTERY TO PLYWOOD BASE.
FASTEN BELL TO PLYWOOD BASE.
TEST RINGING CIRCUIT OF BELL.
SPIN OVERHEAD (OUTSIDE) BY STANDING ON
A CHAIR OR LADDER.
HAVE STUDENTS FORM A 20' DIA. CIRCLE.

VIBRATING HACKSAW BLADE

The number of times a body vibrates per second is called the frequency, and a higher or lower sound is called pitch. If we place the hacksaw blade on the edge of a table and give the knob a downward push, it will vibrate and produce a sound. If we increase the length of the blade that extends over the table, the blade will move further up and down and produce a lower sound, thus illustrating pitch.

The up and down motion of the knob could be related to the wavelength (the distance the vibrating object travels from its normal position of rest). Therefore we can develop the following relationship that exists between wavelength, pitch, and frequency:

1. The longer the wavelength, the lower the frequency.
2. The higher the frequency, the higher the pitch.

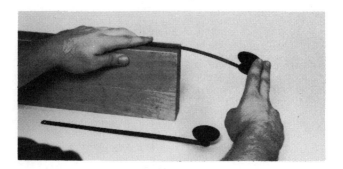

Photo 88

VIBRATING HACKSAW BLADE DIAGRAM 88
FREQUENCY & WAVELENGTH

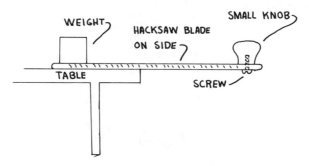

VARY LENGTH OF BLADE EXTENDING BEYOND THE TABLE & COMPARE DISTANCE KNOB TRAVELS & NUMBER OF VIBRATIONS. IMPROVISE SCALE(A RULER WILL DO) & PLACE BEHIND KNOB.

VOCAL CORDS

Vocal cords are membranes in your larynx (Adam's apple —a projection of cartilage in the front of a man's throat). As air from our lungs passes between them, it causes them to vibrate and thus make musical sounds or speech. A variety of sounds are made by changing the tension of your vocal cords and by changing the position of your tongue and lips, over which the sound passes. The vocal cords of girls and children are high-pitched because their vocal cords are short. Longer vocal cords of men vibrate more slowly and therefore make a lower pitch.

By blowing into the tube of the model, the thin membranes are caused to vibrate and produce a sound. Investigations relating to the size of the tube, thickness of the membranes, and space between the membranes provide activities for individual students.

Photo 89

VOCAL CORDS (WORKING MODEL) DIAGRAM 89

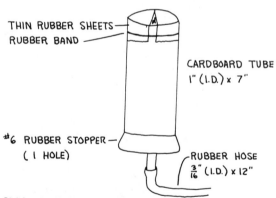

THIN RUBBER SHEETS
RUBBER BAND

CARDBOARD TUBE
1" (I.D.) x 7"

#6 RUBBER STOPPER
(I HOLE)

RUBBER HOSE
$\frac{3}{16}$" (I.D.) x 12"

PLACE THIN RUBBER SHEETS TIGHTLY AND CLOSE
TOGETHER ON ONE END OF CARDBOARD TUBE.
BLOW INTO RUBBER TUBE & RUBBER SHEETS VIBRATE.
ADJUST SPACE BETWEEN RUBBER SHEETS FOR
BEST RESULTS.

chapter 11

Exploring Concepts in Space Science

The science of astronomy, man's oldest science, is about four thousand years old. As man's oldest science, it has practical uses in navigation, surveying, and the study of the weather. When scientists investigate the mysteries of the universe, the heavens are the astronomer's laboratory and the telescope is one of his tools.

Our earth is part of the solar system of nine planets completely at the mercy of the sun. The sun, considered to be an ordinary star in brightness, temperature, and size, provides all the heat and light of the solar system. Also part of the solar system are moons, asteroids, comets, and meteors.

Meteors are particles of stone and iron that travel through space in swarms. Thousands of meteors enter the earth's atmosphere daily, but very few actually strike the earth. Around 1985 we can expect the return of Halley's Comet. This is believed to be made of masses of snow with a sandlike dust mixed in.

A rocket differs from a jet plane in that a rocket's fuel includes all the oxygen needed for combustion while a jet must take in a steady supply of air to keep its fuel burning. The rocket develops a forward pull (thrust) by permitting a stream of high-velocity gases to escape from the exhaust at the rear of the engine.

A variety of demonstrations and models are presented in this chapter that attempt to help students understand the celestial sphere, rockets, the earth's motions, and other concepts related to space science.

THE CELESTIAL SPHERE

An attempt to simplify a difficult concept is the Celestial Sphere model. In reality, the sphere is of infinite radius surrounding the earth and objects in space can be considered as being located on its surface.

The model attempts to illustrate the relationship that exists between the earth and the objects and points in space that are considered occupying a position on the celestial sphere.

It must be remembered that some reference points on the celestial sphere (celestial poles, celestial equator, and hour circles) are based upon the assumption that the center of the earth is the center of the celestial sphere.

In construction, the size of the world globe should again determine the size of the celestial sphere. The identifying circles were made of #10 copper wire and wired together in place with fine copper wire before soldering. Different-colored paints can be used to identify various circles on the sphere. It should be noted that the zenith is not the same position for everyone. The equinoxes and other identified points are labeled and fastened at the correct location on the sphere.

Photo 90

THE CELESTIAL SPHERE DIAGRAM 90

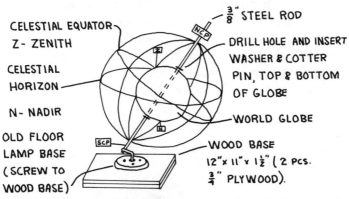

CELESTIAL EQUATOR
Z - ZENITH

CELESTIAL
HORIZON

N - NADIR

OLD FLOOR
LAMP BASE
(SCREW TO
WOOD BASE)

$\frac{3}{8}$" STEEL ROD

DRILL HOLE AND INSERT
WASHER & COTTER
PIN, TOP & BOTTOM
OF GLOBE

WORLD GLOBE

WOOD BASE
12"x 11"x 1$\frac{1}{2}$" (2 PCS.
$\frac{3}{4}$" PLYWOOD).

SIZE OF CELESTIAL SPHERE DEPENDS ON SIZE OF WORLD
GLOBE.
HOUR CIRCLES & OTHER IDENTIFYING CIRCLES MADE FROM
#10 COPPER WIRE.
TIE WIRES TOGETHER WITH FINE COPPER WIRE BEFORE
SOLDERING.
PAINT IDENTIFYING CIRCLES DIFFERENT COLORS &
TYPE LABEL

ASTROLABE

In addition to measuring vertical and horizontal angles as applicable in a math class, the astrolabe can be used for locating objects on the celestial sphere. Using the earth's horizon as a reference point, the astrolabe is used in the azimuth-altitude system of locating stars and planets.

For classroom use, care must be taken to be certain of one's horizontal plane of reference when measuring vertical angles. Students can lay out various geometric combinations outdoors. Such activities include checking the accuracy of the layout of the various fields used for athletic events on school grounds. For extra accuracy, cross-hairs can be glued on the end of the tube, and a 5-foot vertical marker with a 6-inch disc could be constructed and used as an identifying rod marker.

To use the astrolabe, the "0" degree marker on the base is pointed to the direction north. The broom handle is turned manually, while holding the base in its original position, to a point under a star. The tube is then raised to locate the star. This procedure enables us to find the azimuth angle (clockwise direction from north) and the altitude angle (measured from the horizon) of a celestial body.

Photo 91

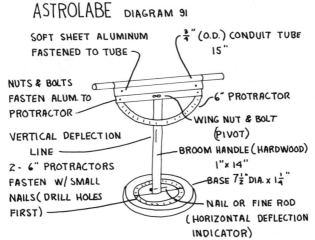

ASTROLABE DIAGRAM 91

SOFT SHEET ALUMINUM   3/4" (O.D.) CONDUIT TUBE
FASTENED TO TUBE   15"

NUTS & BOLTS
FASTEN ALUM. TO
PROTRACTOR

6" PROTRACTOR

WING NUT & BOLT
(PIVOT)

VERTICAL DEFLECTION
LINE

BROOM HANDLE (HARDWOOD)
1" x 14"

2 - 6" PROTRACTORS
FASTEN W/ SMALL
NAILS (DRILL HOLES
FIRST)

BASE 7 1/2" DIA. x 1 1/4"

NAIL OR FINE ROD
(HORIZONTAL DEFLECTION
INDICATOR)

DRILL HOLE IN BASE FOR MOVABLE VERTICAL SUPPORT.
FORM SHEET ALUMINUM AROUND METAL TUBE & BOLT.
DRILL HOLES IN PLASTIC PROTRACTOR TO FASTEN TO
ALUMINUM.
WING NUT & BOLT (PLUS WASHERS) PASS THROUGH
PROTRACTOR AND VERTICAL SUPPORT TO ACT
AS PIVOT.

PLANETS MODEL

Although the planets model is not constructed with relative distance taken into consideration, the model does illustrate the order of the planets in their relative position to each other and to the sun.

It should be explained that scientists classify planets in a number of different ways. "Superior" planets are those farther from the sun than the earth and "inferior" planets are those nearer to the sun than the earth.

The orbits of the planets can be demonstrated by moving each support wire around the center light socket. It must be remembered that the orbits of the planets are elliptical, and this can lead into a demonstration on the chalkboard of an ellipse, using two suction cups and a string.

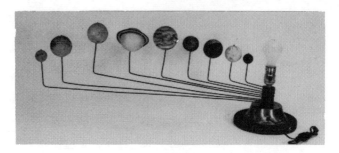

Photo 92

PLANETS MODEL DIAGRAM 92

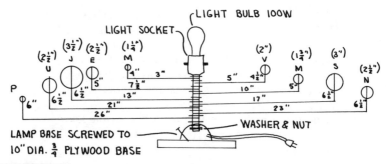

LAMP BASE SCREWED TO
10" DIA. ¾ PLYWOOD BASE

CONSTRUCTION
FORM LOOP AROUND LAMP ROD (THREADED) ⊙———.
USE 1½" STEEL WASHER BETWEEN EACH WIRE SUPPORT.
PLANET SUPPORTS MADE FROM HEAVY COAT HANGER WIRE.
COLOR PLANETS.
MERCURY MADE FROM SMALL SPONGE BALL. ALL OTHERS STYROFOAM.
BEND PLANET SUPPORT WIRES UPWARD' SLIGHTLY, HAVE WIRE GO
THRU PLANETS.

SEASONS MODEL

One of the most useful teaching aids is the seasons model.
The beginning construction should be a class demonstration in
constructing an ellipse on the plywood base. Throughout the
earth's revolution around the sun, the earth's axis of 23½°
points in the same direction.

By painting one half of the tennis ball black, day and night can be easily illustrated. The reason that day and night change in length is that the earth revolves around the sun. There is a gradual change in the amount that each hemisphere leans toward or away from the sun, giving us the seasons.

Using part of the tennis ball seam, both the Arctic and Antarctic Circle can be illuminated by the bulb during the proper seasons. Magic marker colors the spheres quickly and a 100 watt bulb is recommended. It is further suggested that the model be left on display, because it illustrates too many concepts for one or two lessons to be mastered.

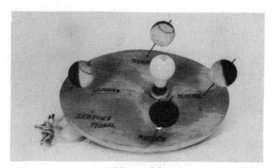

Photo 93

SEASONS MODEL DIAGRAM 93

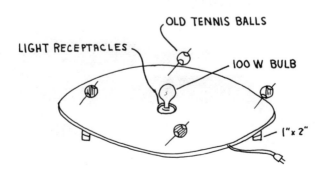

BASE -- $\frac{3}{4}$"x 18"x 16" PLYWOOD.
USE OLD TENNIS BALLS COLORED WITH MARKER.
USE HEAVY COAT HANGER WIRE. PUNCH HOLES &
PUSH THRU TENNIS BALLS.
BEND WIRES TO APPROX. 23°.
DRILL HOLES FOR WIRE. (MAKE HOLES TIGHT.)
DRILL HOLES TO SHOW PERIHELION & APHELION.

ACTION-REACTION ACCELERATION

Illustrating Newton's third law of motion is easily accomplished by taping a CO_2 cartridge to a flat car resting on "0" gauge Lionel train tracks. The cartridge is punctured with a spring-driven needle. The car is propelled forward while the compressed gas is discharged backward. It must be remembered that forward motion (reaction) is a result of the gas being discharged backward (action).

With the car traveling over a measured distance, the speed can be calculated in mph. Various weights can be added to the car and a graph drawn comparing the speed to the mass of the car.

Another innovation is the fastening of a timer and tape to the car. The students can measure distances between the dots on the tape at various locations along the track.

CO_2 cartridges and plunger are obtainable at large home-improvement stores in the bar supplies and equipment department, as well as at hobby shops.

Photo 94

ACTION-REACTION and ACCELERATION DIAGRAM 94

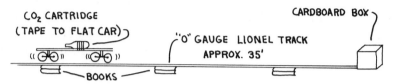

CO₂ CARTRIDGE
(TAPE TO FLAT CAR)

CARDBOARD BOX

"O" GAUGE LIONEL TRACK
APPROX. 35'

BOOKS

BOOKS ON BOTH SIDES OF TRACK TO HOLD TRACK IN PLACE.
RECOMMEND USE ON FLOOR APPROX. 35'.
CATCH CAR IN CARDBOARD BOX.
MEASURE TIME AND COMPUTE M.P.H.
TIMER & TAPE MAY BE USED FOR ACCELERATION MEASUREMENTS.

ACTION-REACTION BICYCLE WHEEL

Another demonstration illustrating Newton's third law of motion is performed using a 16″ bicycle wheel mounted inversely on a wooden base. After the tire is removed, the CO_2 cartridge is taped to the rim and punctured with a spring-driven needle.

Photo 95

Using the measurement of the diameter of the wheel and averaging the number of rotations per given time, the speed can be computed in mph. In addition, a graph can be drawn plotting the rpm's against the various time segments to illustrate the acceleration and deceleration curve. It is recommended that a lightweight aluminum wheel with a diameter of approximately 16″ be used. It is also important to lubricate the bearings to reduce the friction.

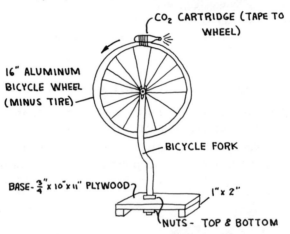

ACTION-REACTION   DIAGRAM 95

CO₂ CARTRIDGE (TAPE TO WHEEL)

16″ ALUMINUM BICYCLE WHEEL (MINUS TIRE)

BICYCLE FORK

BASE- ¾″ x 10″ x 11″ PLYWOOD

1″ x 2″

NUTS - TOP & BOTTOM

USE CO₂ PLUNGER TO ACTIVATE WHEEL.
COMPUTE WHEEL CIRCUMFERENCE, AVERAGE R.P.M.'s,
& CONVERT TO M.P.H.

GYRO

The gyro concept demonstrated by the bicycle wheel illustrates how a wheel or disc maintains a fixed axis of rotation. The student rides his bicycle and can maintain an upright position as long as sufficient speed is maintained.

A horizontal axis can be maintained by spinning the wheel manually and holding the wheel suspended with the cord or having it rest on the demonstrator's fingers. Another experience is to have a student grasp the aluminum handles, walk briskly, and attempt to make a 180° turn with the wheel spinning. The gyroscopic inertia can be felt by the wheel's resistance to the change of direction.

A tire on the wheel inflated to its capacity pressure aids in the demonstration's effectiveness. Gyroscopes are used in many aircraft, rockets, and stabilizing instruments.

Photo 96

THE GYRO   DIAGRAM 96

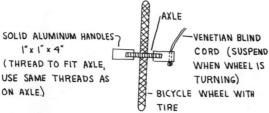

SOLID ALUMINUM HANDLES
1"x 1" x 4"
(THREAD TO FIT AXLE,
USE SAME THREADS AS
ON AXLE.)

AXLE

VENETIAN BLIND
CORD (SUSPEND
WHEN WHEEL IS
TURNING)

BICYCLE WHEEL WITH
TIRE

USE A 16" WHEEL FOR SMALL STUDENTS & 24" WHEEL FOR BIG STUDENTS.
INFLATE TIRE.
THE WHEEL CAN BE SUSPENDED FROM THE CHORD WHEN IT IS GIVEN A HARD TURN.
STUDENTS COULD HOLD BOTH HANDLES AND WALK, THEN TURN TO FEEL THE EFFECT OF THE SPINNING WHEEL.
BE SURE ALL NUTS ARE ON AXLE BEFORE TURNING ON ALUMINUM HANDLES.

ROCKET MODELS

Excellent classroom displays and student problem solving activities can be initiated by rocket designs limited to inexpensive and easily obtainable materials. The most common and available materials are cardboard tubes which can be assembled in a variety of ways using tape, wire, or glue.

A variety of rocket models can be constructed. Some cutaway views showing the fuel and combustion chambers of liquid fuel as well as solid fuel rockets are well within the range of most students and well covered in most reference books. It is suggested that some relationship be developed between the rockets and the CO_2 demonstrations listed in this book. This book illustrates only a few of the many possibilities.

Photo 97   **Photo 98**

SATURN ROCKET MODEL DIAGRAM 97

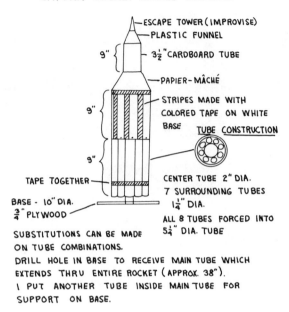

ESCAPE TOWER (IMPROVISE)
PLASTIC FUNNEL
9" $3\frac{1}{2}$" CARDBOARD TUBE

PAPIER-MÂCHÉ

STRIPES MADE WITH
COLORED TAPE ON WHITE
9" BASE

TUBE CONSTRUCTION

9"

TAPE TOGETHER

CENTER TUBE 2" DIA.
7 SURROUNDING TUBES
$1\frac{1}{4}$" DIA.

BASE - 10" DIA.
$\frac{3}{4}$" PLYWOOD

ALL 8 TUBES FORCED INTO
$5\frac{1}{4}$" DIA. TUBE

SUBSTITUTIONS CAN BE MADE
ON TUBE COMBINATIONS.
DRILL HOLE IN BASE TO RECEIVE MAIN TUBE WHICH
EXTENDS THRU ENTIRE ROCKET (APPROX. 38").
I PUT ANOTHER TUBE INSIDE MAIN TUBE FOR
SUPPORT ON BASE.

TITAN ROCKET MODEL DIAGRAM 98

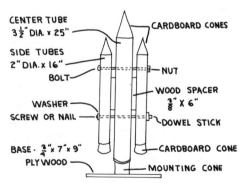

CENTER TUBE
$3\frac{1}{2}$" DIA. x 25"

CARDBOARD CONES

SIDE TUBES
2" DIA. x 16"

BOLT

NUT

WOOD SPACER
$\frac{3}{8}$" X 6"

WASHER
SCREW OR NAIL

DOWEL STICK

BASE - $\frac{3}{4}$" x 7" x 9"
PLYWOOD

CARDBOARD CONE
MOUNTING CONE

DRILL HOLE IN BASE TO FIT MOUNTING CONE.
DOWEL STICKS CAN BE SUBSTITUTED FOR BOLTS.
USE SMALLER CONES ON SMALLER TUBES.
GLUE CONES ON TUBES.

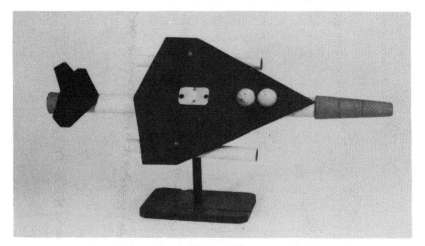

Photo 99

RAM JET MODEL   DIAGRAM 99

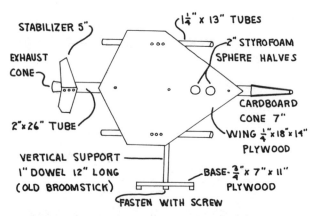

STABILIZER 5"

EXHAUST
CONE

2"x 26" TUBE

VERTICAL SUPPORT
1" DOWEL 12" LONG
(OLD BROOMSTICK)

FASTEN WITH SCREW

$1\frac{1}{4}$" x 13" TUBES

2" STYROFOAM
SPHERE HALVES

CARDBOARD
CONE 7"

WING $\frac{1}{4}$"x 18"x 19"
PLYWOOD

BASE- $\frac{3}{4}$" x 7"x 11"
PLYWOOD

MOUNT MODEL AT APPROX. 45° ANGLE ON VERTICAL
SUPPORT.
PARTS CAN BE WIRED TOGETHER OR USE LONG BOLTS.
SUBSTITUTIONS IN SIZE & SHAPE ARE ACCEPTABLE.
USE GLUE TO HOLD CONES IN PLACE.
GLUE 2 STYROFOAM HALVES FOR COCKPIT.

Photo 100

NUCLEAR ROCKET MODEL DIAGRAM 100

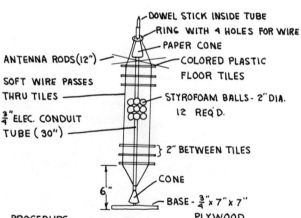

DOWEL STICK INSIDE TUBE
RING WITH 4 HOLES FOR WIRE
PAPER CONE
COLORED PLASTIC FLOOR TILES
ANTENNA RODS(12")
SOFT WIRE PASSES THRU TILES
STYROFOAM BALLS - 2" DIA. 12 REQ'D.
$\frac{3}{4}$" ELEC. CONDUIT TUBE (30")
} 2" BETWEEN TILES
CONE
6"
BASE - $\frac{3}{4}$" x 7" x 7" PLYWOOD

PROCEDURE

DRILL HOLES IN 4 CORNERS OF EACH PLASTIC TILE.
DRILL HOLE IN CENTER OF EACH TILE TO FIT TUBE.
PLACE TILES 2" APART.
DRILL TIGHT HOLE IN BASE TO SUPPORT TUBE.
PASS WIRE THRU STYROFOAM BALLS & WIRE TO TUBE.
DRILL HOLES IN TUBE FOR ANTENNA RODS.
ASSEMBLE ROCKET BEFORE MAKING POSITIONS
OF PARTS PERMANENT (VARIATIONS ACCEPTABLE).

SUNDIAL

The sundial is the oldest known device for the measurement of time. It is based on the fact that the shadow of an object will move from one side of the object to the other as the sun moves from the east to the west during the day.

The sundial tells time by measuring the angle of a shadow cast by the sun. A flat piece of material, called a gnomen, is fastened in the center of the dial. When the sun's rays hit the gnomen it casts a shadow, and this shadow indicates the time of day.

The basic parts of the sundial are the flat plane (face) on which are inscribed the hour divisions. The gnomen points toward the North Pole in the Northern Hemisphere and toward the South Pole in the Southern Hemisphere. The angle of the gnomen must correspond to an angle equal to the observer's latitude. Consideration must be taken for weather conditions and daylight savings time.

Photo 101

SUN DIAL DIAGRAM 101

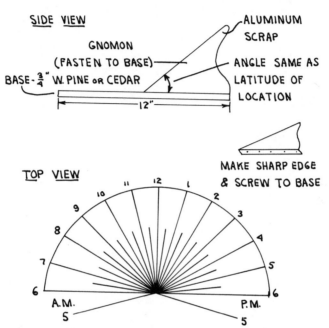

SIDE VIEW

ALUMINUM SCRAP

GNOMON
(FASTEN TO BASE)——

BASE- $\frac{3}{4}$" W. PINE or CEDAR

ANGLE SAME AS
LATITUDE OF
LOCATION

|——— 12" ———|

MAKE SHARP EDGE
& SCREW TO BASE

TOP VIEW

10 11 12 1

9   2

8   3

7   4

6   5

6

A.M.   P.M.

5   5

FASTEN GNOMON FROM CENTER ON 12 NOON LINE.
POINT GNOMON TO NORTH POLE.
EACH HOUR = 15°.

chapter 12

Challenging Activities
for Everyone

This chapter illustrates some teaching aids that required considerable experimentation before satisfactory results were obtained. The glass-jug cutter proved difficult because of the uneven thickness of the glass jug. The importance of a good score mark was finally obtained by oiling the cutting wheel.

The cost of math solids was the motivation for experimentation with a variety of materials. Plastic tiles obtained from a floor covering store proved a satisfactory substitute. The tiles are easily workable with power tools and contact cement. The focus here is on size—the same amount of work is involved in constructing a 2-inch model as there is in constructing a 6-inch model. The durability exceeds commercial models.

The probability demonstrator represents a student project. The idea, obtained from a sourcebook, was completed successfully by substituting yardsticks for the slot construction. The spheres are easily collected after use by lifting the slots off the board and pouring the spheres into a container.

The window shade charts provide lasting illustrations of basic concepts in addition to solving the storage problem. Easily obtainable and easily mounted, the window shade charts provide instant use and are applicable in all subject matter areas. A clear, smooth, white plastic window shade can be used as a screen for film and filmstrip projections.

The teaching machine represents a personal experiment in programmed instruction. Although inexpensive to construct, the program involves considerable revisions of subject matter before a satisfactory program can be developed. Students can write their own program on index cards. The device provides easy use and reference.

GLASS-JUG CUTTER

The glass-jug cutter is essentially a hot-wire device that consists of a piece of coiled nichrome wire connected to short pieces of insulated wire that are attached to a male plug. The nichrome wire can be obtained from discarded electrical appliances and should be used in its coiled form.

The apparatus consists of a frame on which the glass is scored with a glass cutter fastened to the base. The glass is rotated and a clean score mark should result. The jug is now placed in the hole in the table and the nichrome wire placed against the score mark. The plug is inserted into an outlet, the wires get hot, and the glass should break cleanly at the score mark. It is suggested that a variac be used and experimentation can help to determine the amount of voltage input necessary. Caution must also be taken that the nichrome wire placed around the jug be separated to prevent a short circuit. This can be done by inserting a piece of yardstick between the two wires.

Glassware is usually fire-polished, but it is further suggested that emery paper on a wood block be used to file off any rough edges. Safety glasses should be worn at all times.

Safety glasses should be worn at all times by anyone in the immediate vicinity as well as by the person doing the demonstration.

Photo 102

GLASS JUG CUTTER DIAGRAM 102

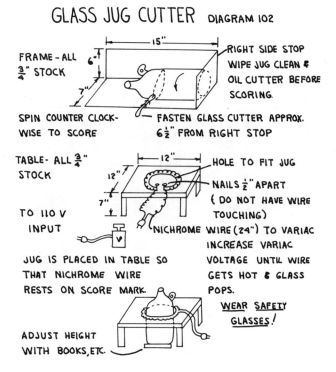

FRAME - ALL $\frac{3}{4}$" STOCK

15"

RIGHT SIDE STOP
WIPE JUG CLEAN &
OIL CUTTER BEFORE
SCORING.

6"

7"

SPIN COUNTER CLOCK-
WISE TO SCORE

FASTEN GLASS CUTTER APPROX.
$6\frac{1}{2}$" FROM RIGHT STOP

TABLE- ALL $\frac{3}{4}$" STOCK

12"

12"

HOLE TO FIT JUG

NAILS $\frac{1}{2}$" APART
(DO NOT HAVE WIRE
TOUCHING)

7"

TO 110 V
INPUT

NICHROME WIRE (24") TO VARIAC
INCREASE VARIAC
VOLTAGE UNTIL WIRE
GETS HOT & GLASS
POPS.

JUG IS PLACED IN TABLE SO
THAT NICHROME WIRE
RESTS ON SCORE MARK.

WEAR SAFETY
GLASSES!

ADJUST HEIGHT
WITH BOOKS, ETC.

MATH SOLIDS

The math solids illustrated were constructed from ⅛" vinyl floor tiles. The tiles were cut on a table saw and after the rough edges were sanded off, the pieces were glued together with contact cement. The name of the solids plus the formulas for finding the area and volume of the solids could be written on the faces with a fine-point marker.

Some solids that can be constructed are listed below:

Cube
Triangular prism
Rectangular prism
Sphere (old softball)
Tetrahedron
Cylinder (linoleum glued on a cardboard tube)
Trapezoid
Pyramid
Octahedron

Photo 103

MATH SOLIDS DIAGRAM 103

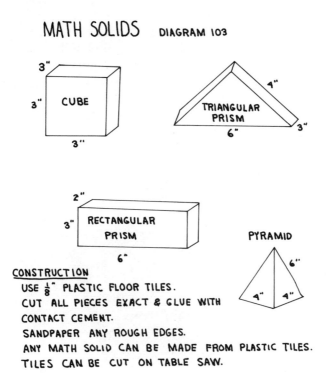

CONSTRUCTION

USE $\frac{1}{8}$" PLASTIC FLOOR TILES.

CUT ALL PIECES EXACT & GLUE WITH

CONTACT CEMENT.

SANDPAPER ANY ROUGH EDGES.

ANY MATH SOLID CAN BE MADE FROM PLASTIC TILES.

TILES CAN BE CUT ON TABLE SAW.

PROBABILITY

The probability model is based upon the type of pinball machine that Galton used in his experiment of a normal probability curve. The construction of the apparatus is considerably simplified by using ⅛″ yardsticks to construct the reception slots. Glass marbles (approximately 15 mm diameter) were substituted for steel balls.

The reception slots should not be fastened permanently to the plywood base. This permits the marbles to be removed easily by lifting the slots and pouring the marbles into a container. The model can be raised at one end by placing a few books under the base to the desired height.

After a number of "runs" of the marbles, produce a pattern that gives an approximation of a normal probability curve.

The model illustrates a degree of regularity that occurs when large masses of measurements are taken. It presents a picture of how the measurements are distributed.

(Ref.—*Sourcebook for Biological Sciences,* Harcourt, Brace, & World, 1966, p. 409.)

Photo 104

PROBABILITY   DIAGRAM 104

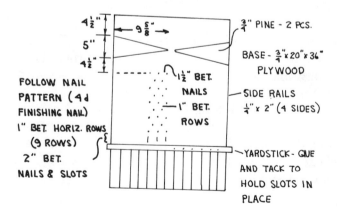

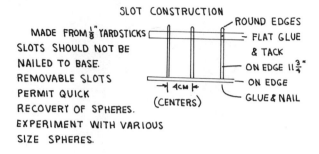

SLOT CONSTRUCTION

MADE FROM ⅛" YARDSTICKS
SLOTS SHOULD NOT BE
NAILED TO BASE.
REMOVABLE SLOTS
PERMIT QUICK
RECOVERY OF SPHERES.
EXPERIMENT WITH VARIOUS
SIZE SPHERES.

ROUND EDGES
FLAT GLUE
& TACK
ON EDGE 11¾"
ON EDGE
GLUE & NAIL

4CM
(CENTERS)

WINDOW SHADE CHARTS

Inexpensive and permanent charts of basic lessons can easily be compiled by utilizing window shades. The procedure used is to project the desired picture or diagram (using the opaque projector, filmstrip projector, or slide projector) on the window shade. Lines can be illustrated by using fine or heavy permanent markers. Coloring, if desired, can be done using colored pencils. Excellent results were obtained by using Venus Paradise colored pencils.

The chart is easily suspended by two eyehooks that are screwed into a ¾" x 2" x 36" piece of wood. The window shade is mounted on the piece of wood by using window shade brackets. Storage is simplified if the same size window shades are used because only one mounting board is necessary.

Window shades are made of a wide variety of materials. The smooth, white, and plain (non-textured) surface shade provides the best results.

Some ideas of permanent charts are listed below:

Electrical diagrams
Contour maps
Graphs
Chemical valences
Geometric diagrams and formulas
Maps

Photo 105

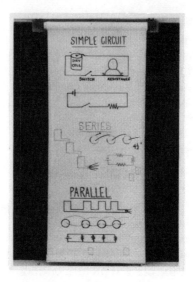

WINDOW SHADE CHARTS DIAGRAM 105

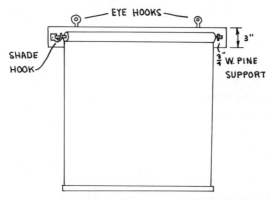

LENGTH OF SUPPORT VARIES WITH LENGTH & WIDTH
OF WINDOW SHADE.
CLEAN PLASTIC SHADES CAN BE USED AS SCREENS.
USE PERMANENT MARKERS & ALLOW TO DRY
THOROUGHLY BEFORE ROLLING UP.
USES - CHARTS- DIAGRAMS - SCREENS
RECOMMEND PLASTIC SHADES & PERMANENT
MARKERS.
OLD SHADE CAN BE WASHED BEFORE USING.

TEACHING MACHINE

A teaching machine is a mechanical device that presents an ordered sequence of instruction to the learner one frame at a time. The program is the body of information presented by the teaching machine. Psychological theory states that the presentation of information in small bits is readily understood by a learner and that a correct response constitutes a psychological reward. The device also permits the student to proceed through the program at his own speed.

The organization of the project can focus on one teaching unit in one grade level or any combination of both. Mechanical construction as illustrated is relatively simple and inexpensive, but difficulty is met in writing the sequential program. This can be resolved by a group of teachers who teach the same subject or a combination of students and teachers.

The typing of the cards can be handled by the typing class after the program is completed. It is suggested that the program contain a variety of required responses, such as would be required on a normal exam.

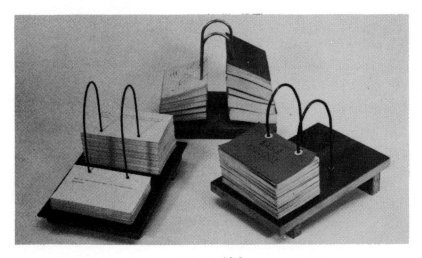

Photo 106

TEACHING MACHINE DIAGRAM 106

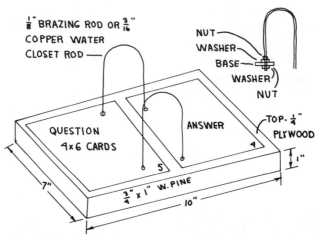

$\frac{1}{8}$" BRAZING ROD OR $\frac{3}{16}$"
COPPER WATER
CLOSET ROD —

NUT —
WASHER —
BASE —
WASHER
NUT

QUESTION
4×6 CARDS

ANSWER

TOP- $\frac{1}{4}$"
PLYWOOD

5

7"

$\frac{3}{4}$" × 1" W.PINE

10"

1"

A 12" ROD WILL ACCOMMODATE 400 CARDS.
DRILL 100 CARDS ON DRILL PRESS AT ONE TIME.
TYPE ANSWER ON BACK OF QUESTION CARD SO
THAT IT CAN BE READ WHEN TURNED OVER.
STUDENTS CAN WRITE OWN PROGRAMS.

Index

Index